I0489497

NUDE: Cali 2 – Playing At Peter's House

Glamour Nude and Erotica Photography Vol. 14

By Peter Dickem

Experience the joy and freedom of releasing all your inhibitions and embracing a nude and erotic life style. Enjoy this amazing and exclusive collection of nude and erotic fine art photography by artist Peter Dickem for **www.peterdickem.com** and **Chameleon Productions**. Featuring the enhanced color eBook layout and high quality photography.

Get motivated and into a great mood today by joining CALI as she shows off her body and bares it all for you to see. The photography is fantastic and there are no words strong enough to describe the effects of the pure beauty and uninhibited attitude of CALI in these 38 explicit glamour and erotic nude photographs.

Collect all the eBooks from the **www.peterdickem.com** collection.

This is Volume 14 in the series of eBooks that showcase some of the many girls from **www.peterdickem.com** and **Chameleon Productions** with more books coming weekly. You can find them by searching Nudes photographed by Peter Dickem in your digital bookstore under Glamour Nudes today.

All of the girls that are seen in this and other photo book series can be seen in their live action videos at one of Peter Dickem's 4 sites on line. They are www.peterdickem.com, www.amateurdreamers.com, www.candypixxx.com and www.oralarizona.com.

CALI
DOB = 04/20/1982   Height = 5'2"
Weight = 100 lbs.   Hair = Blond
Eyes = Brown   Hometown = San Jose, Calif.
Loves sex and being naked.
Her favorite sex position is doggy style.
Hobbies: skate boarding, sex
3 Words to Describe Yourself: horny, horny, and horny.
Favorite Fantasy: having sex in a bar, on a pool table with people watching.

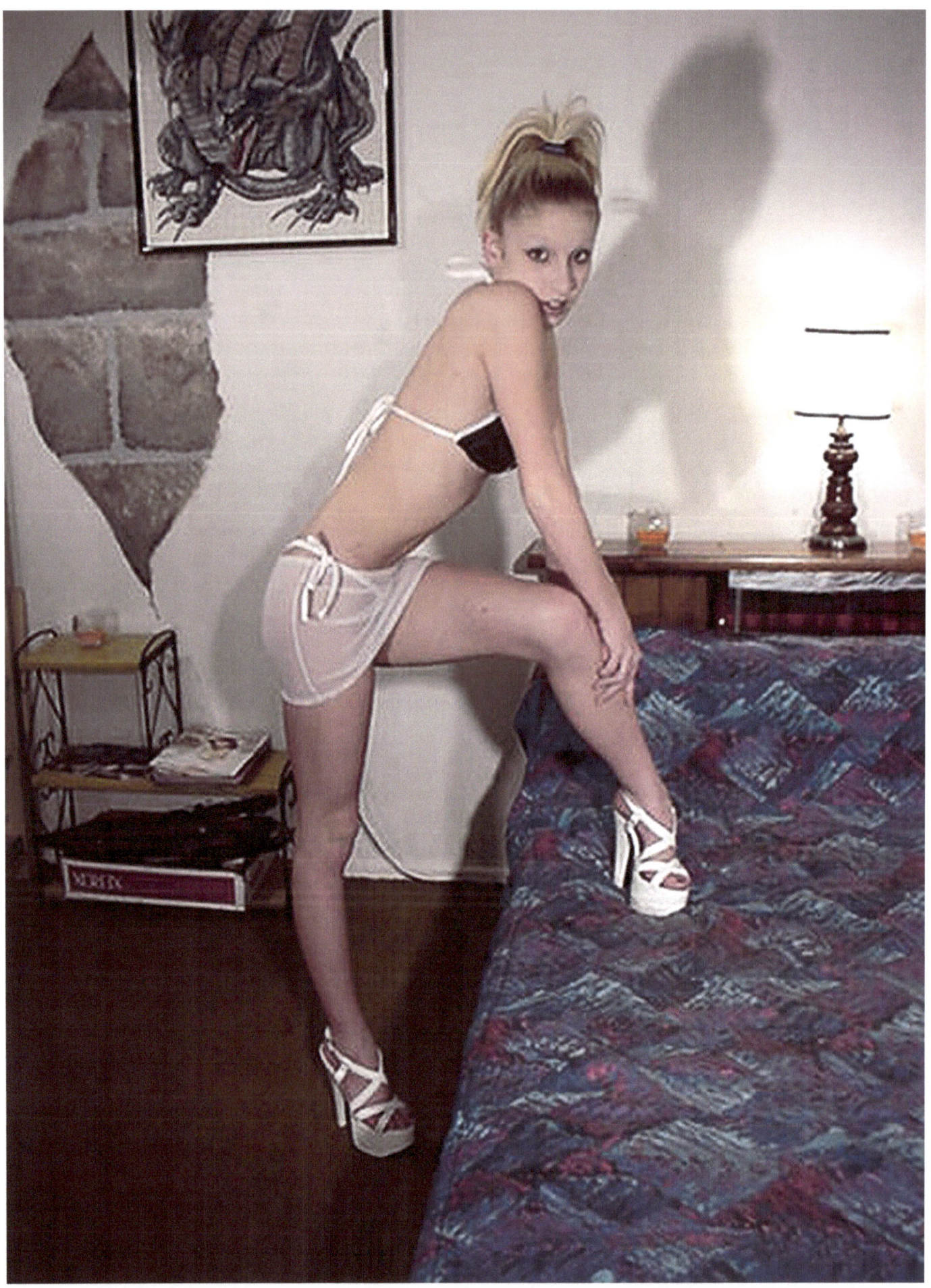

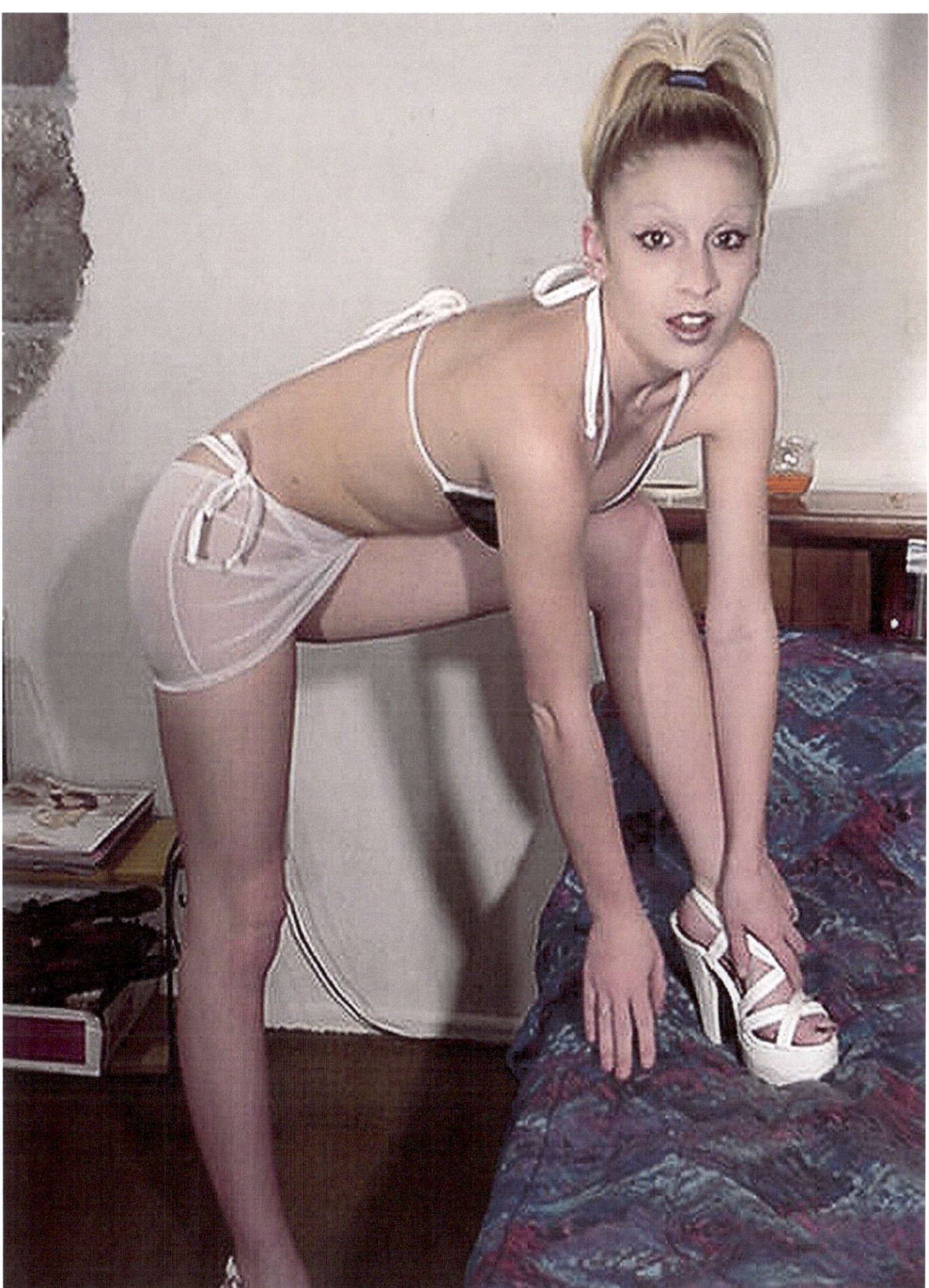

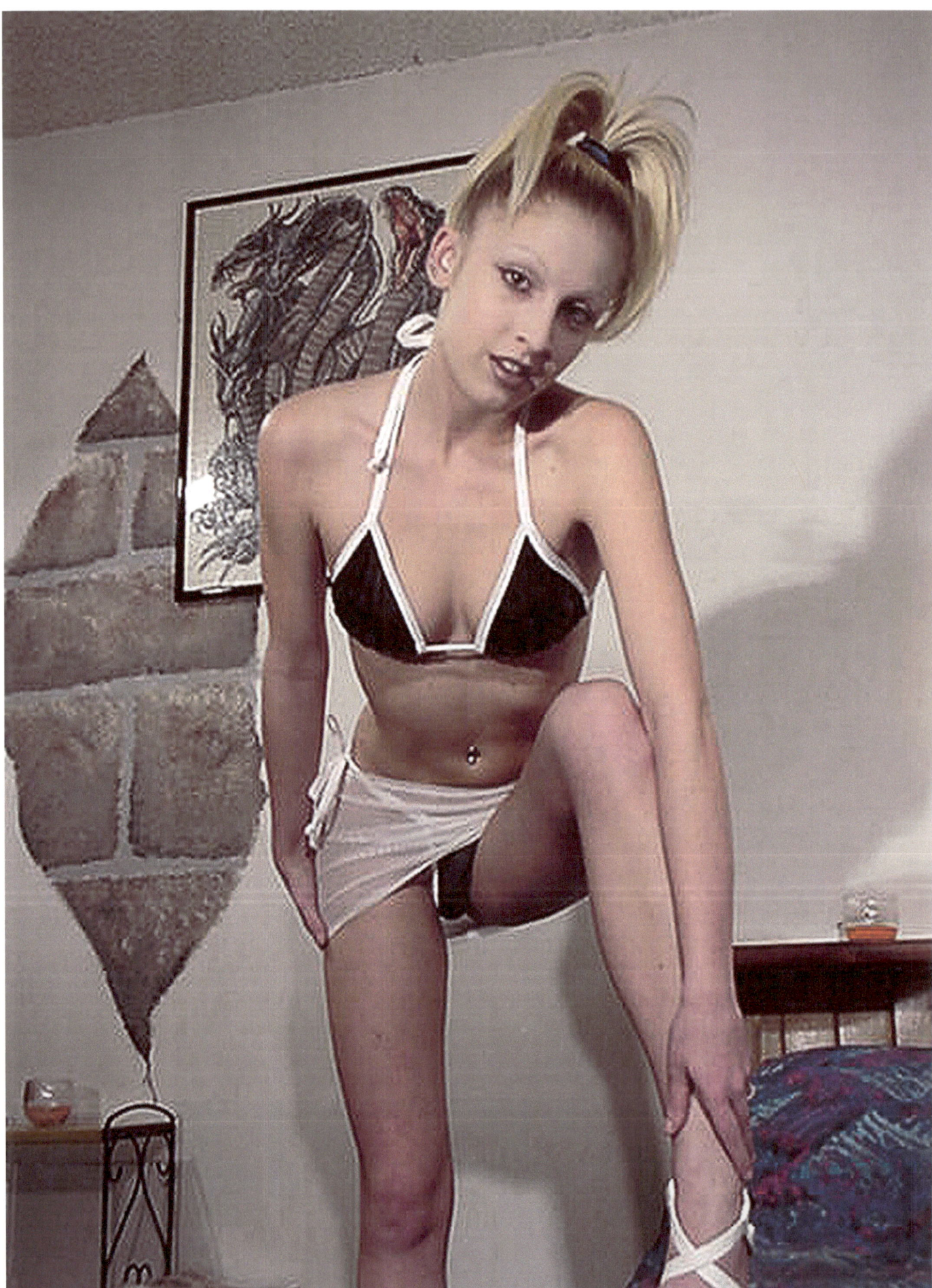

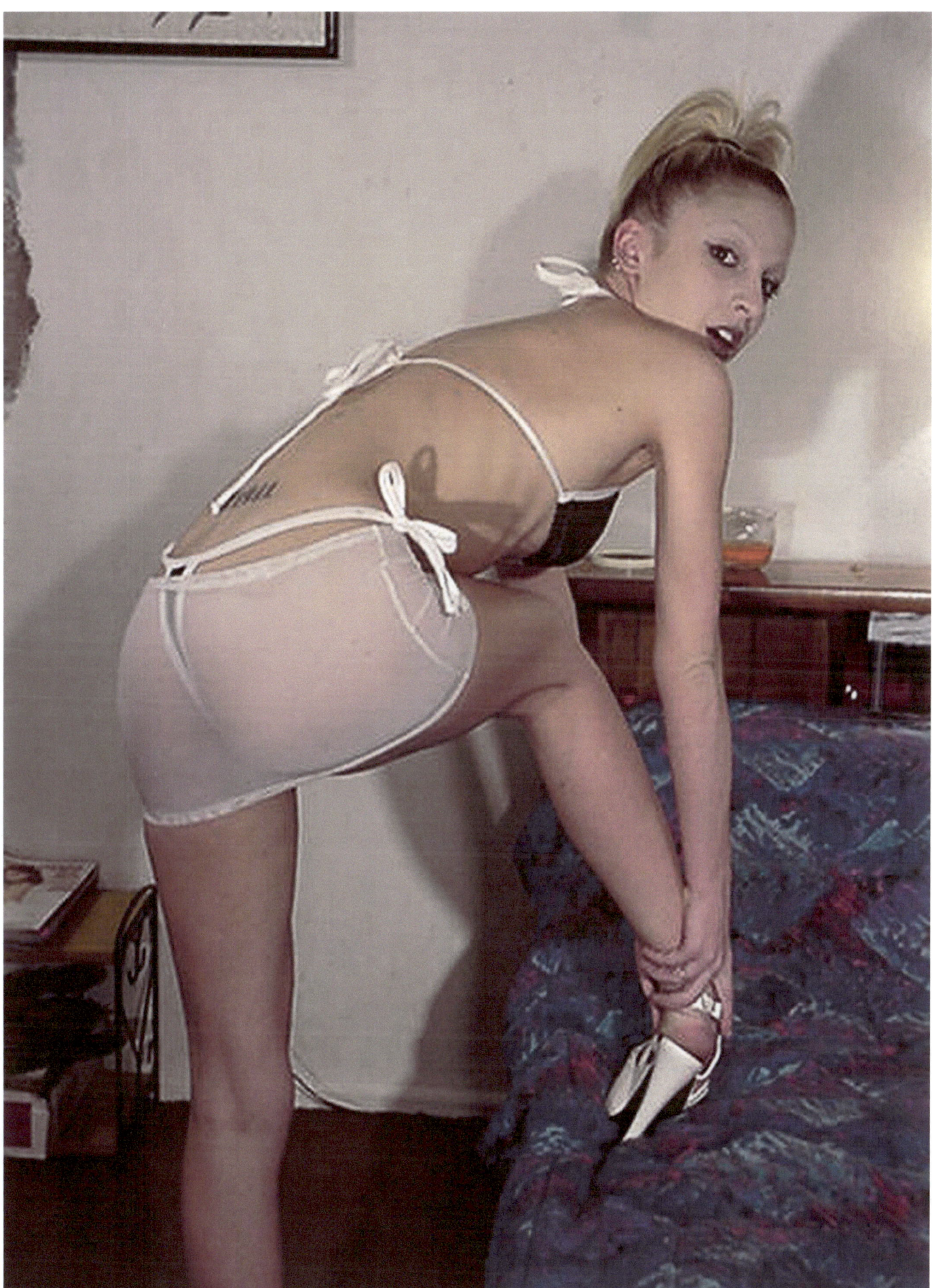

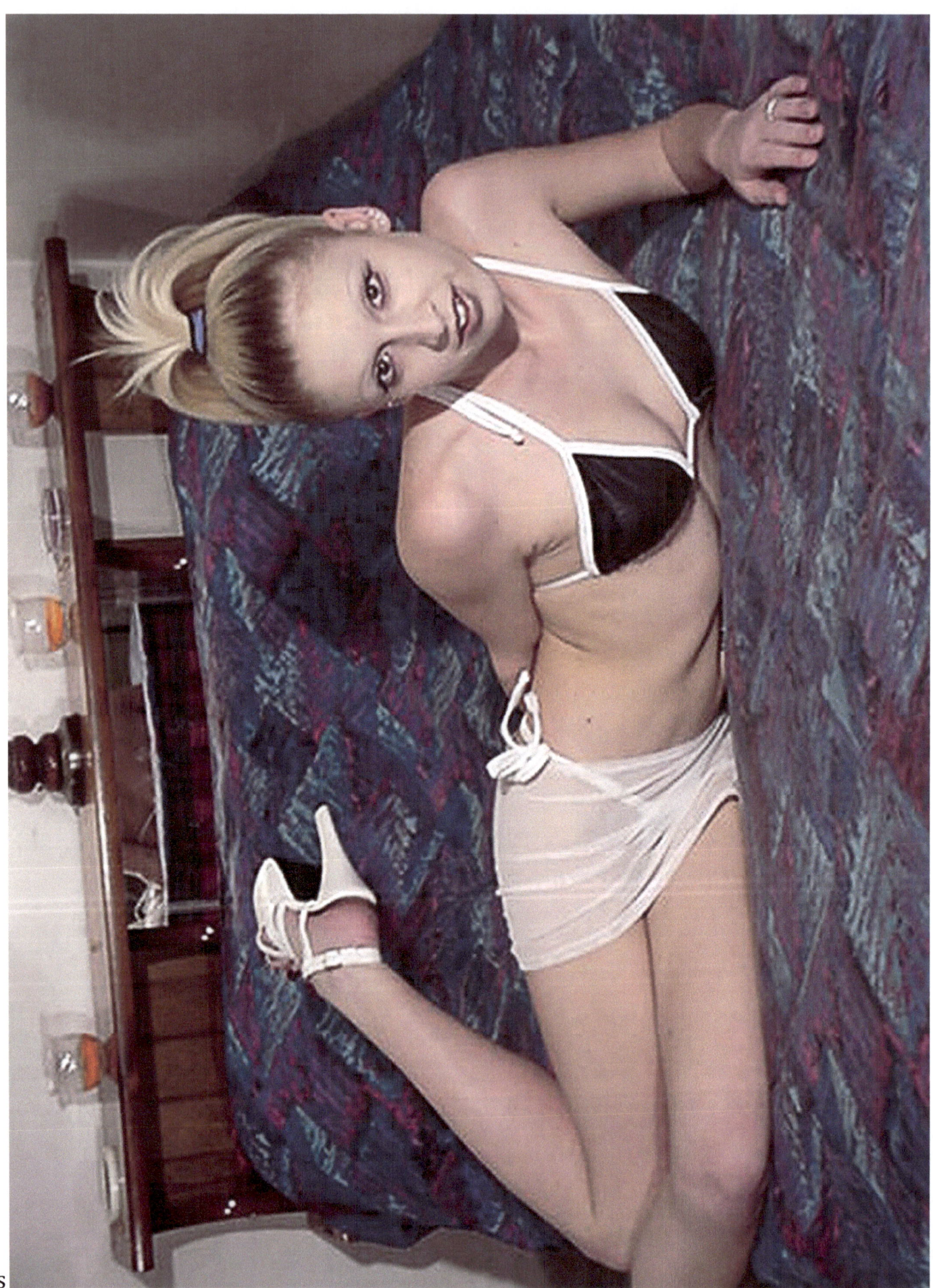

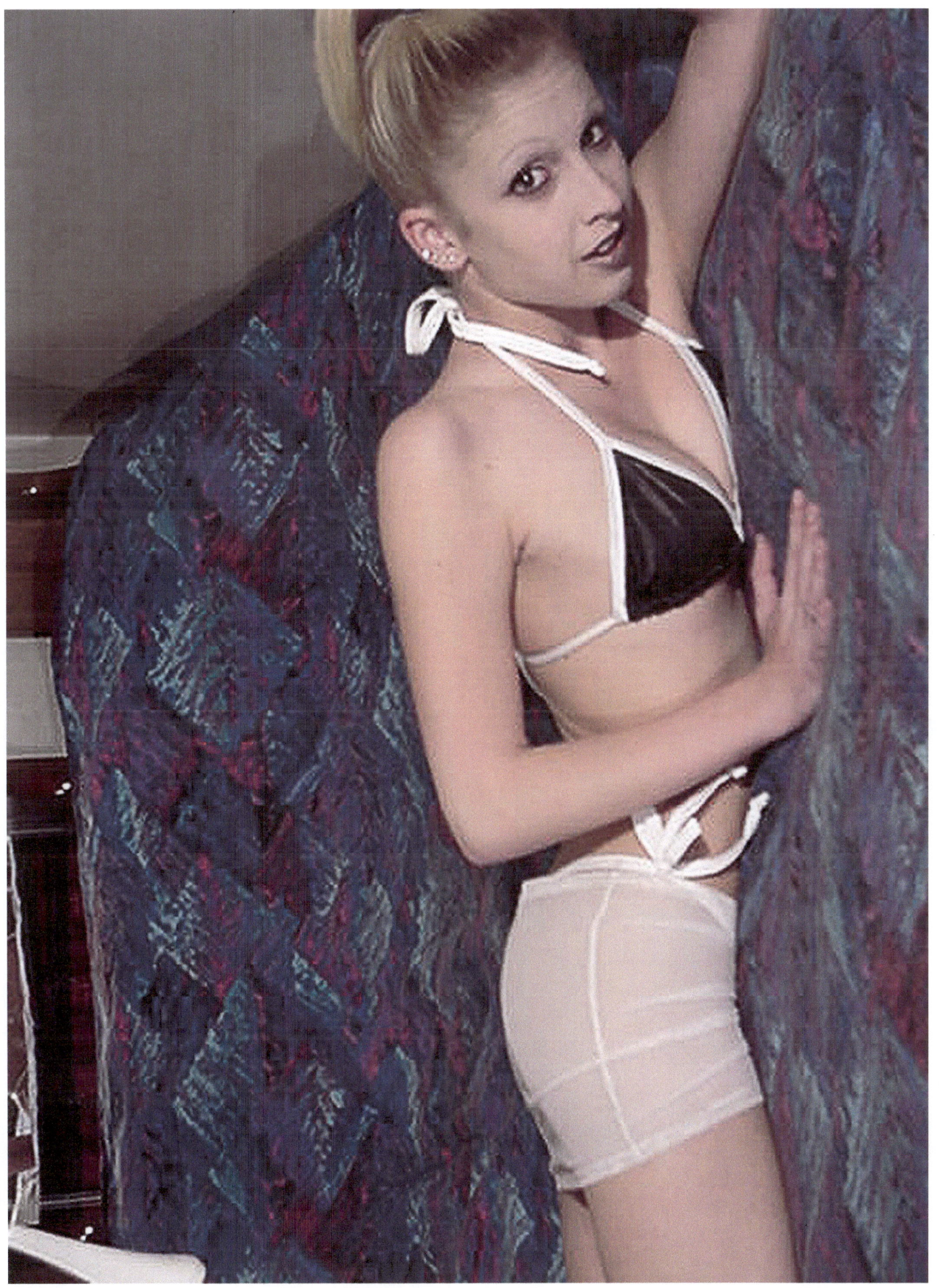

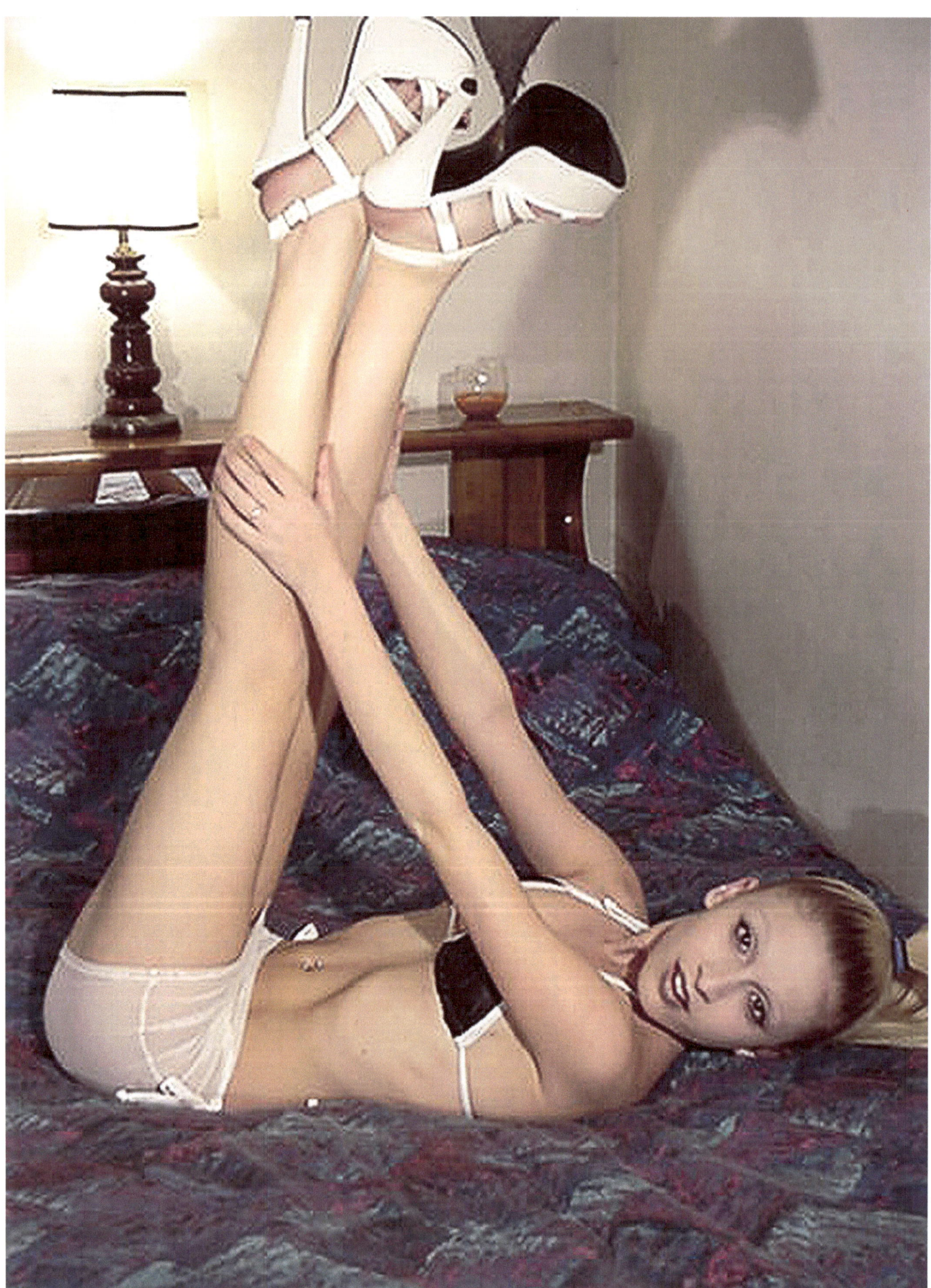

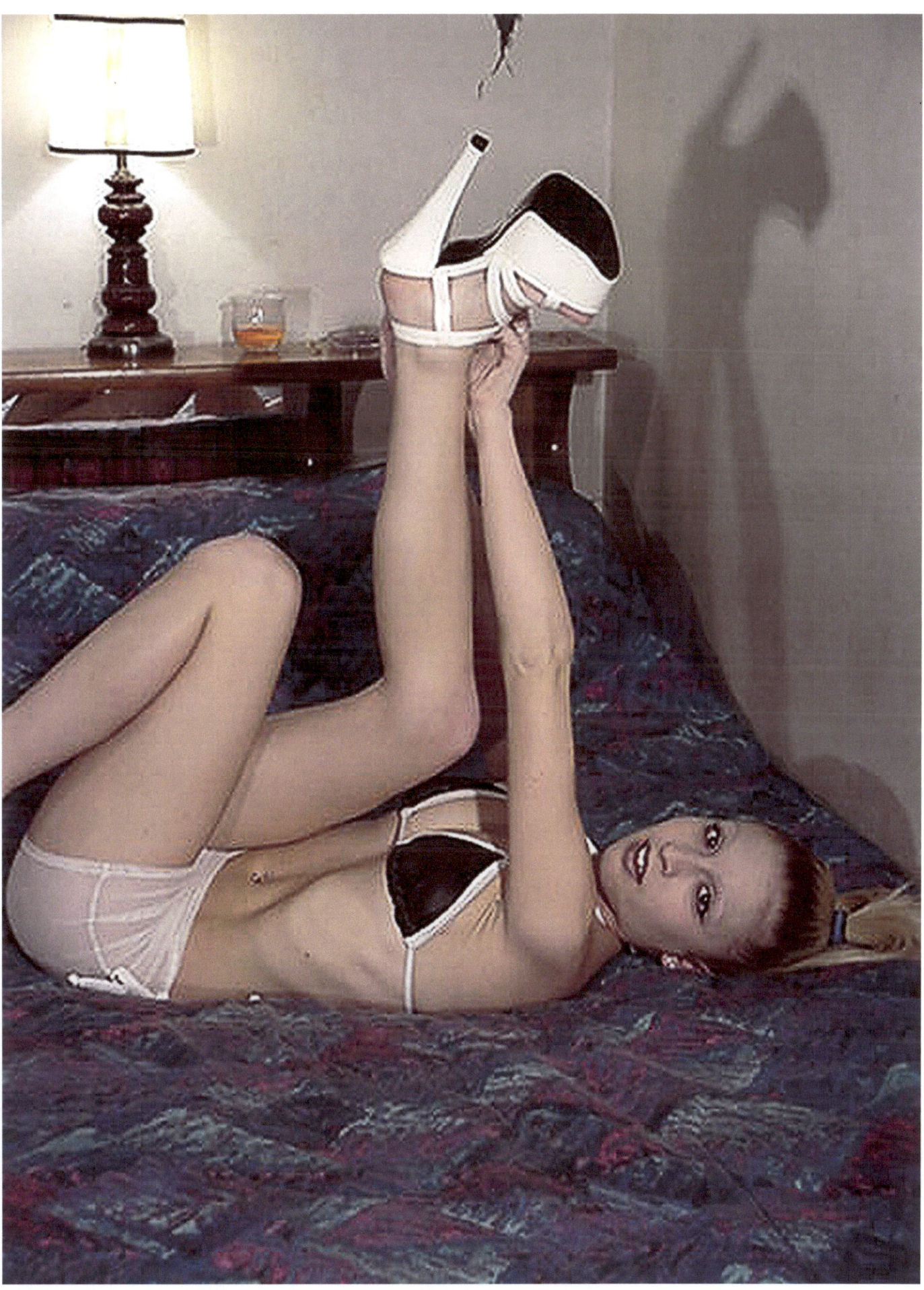

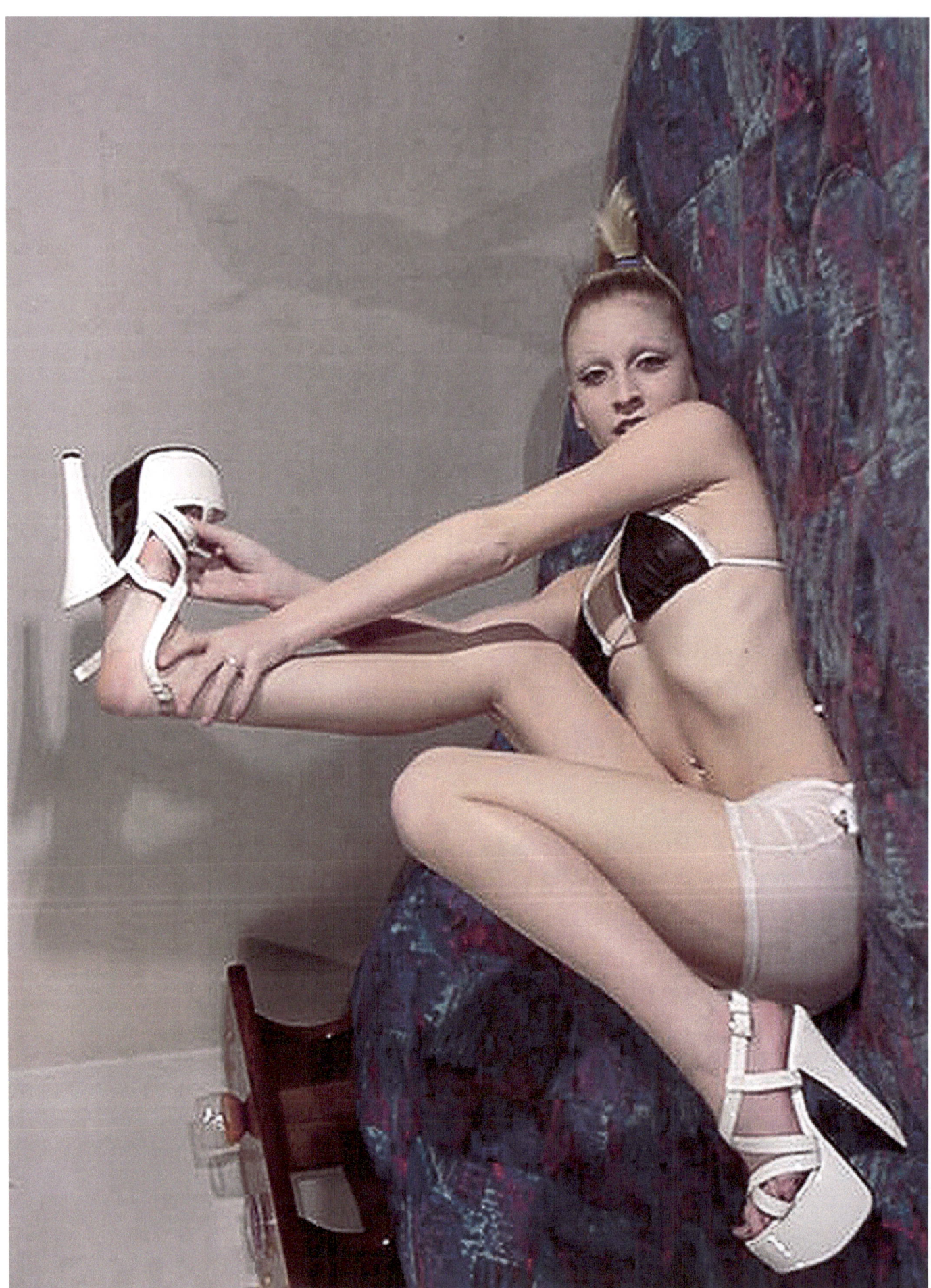

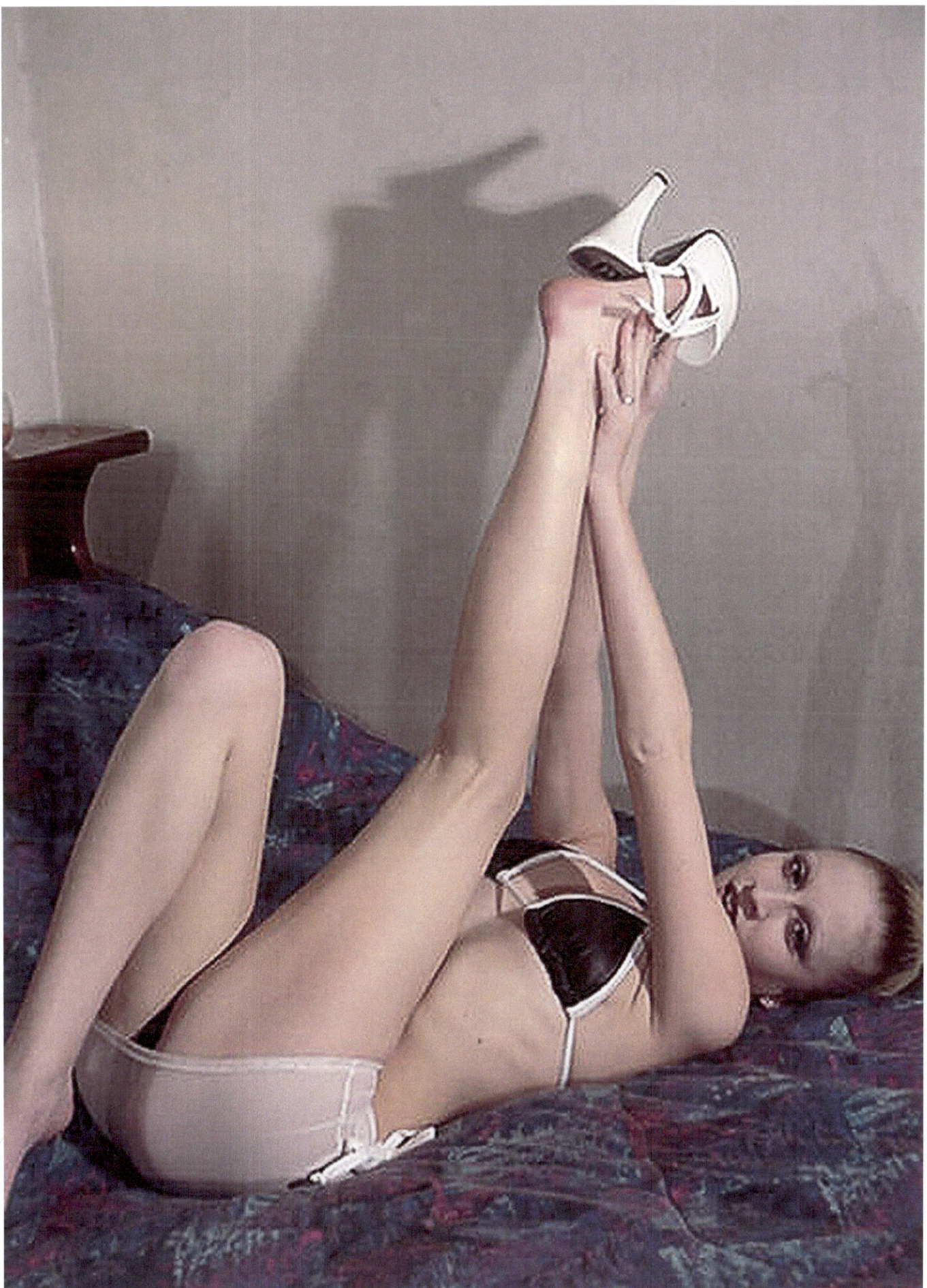

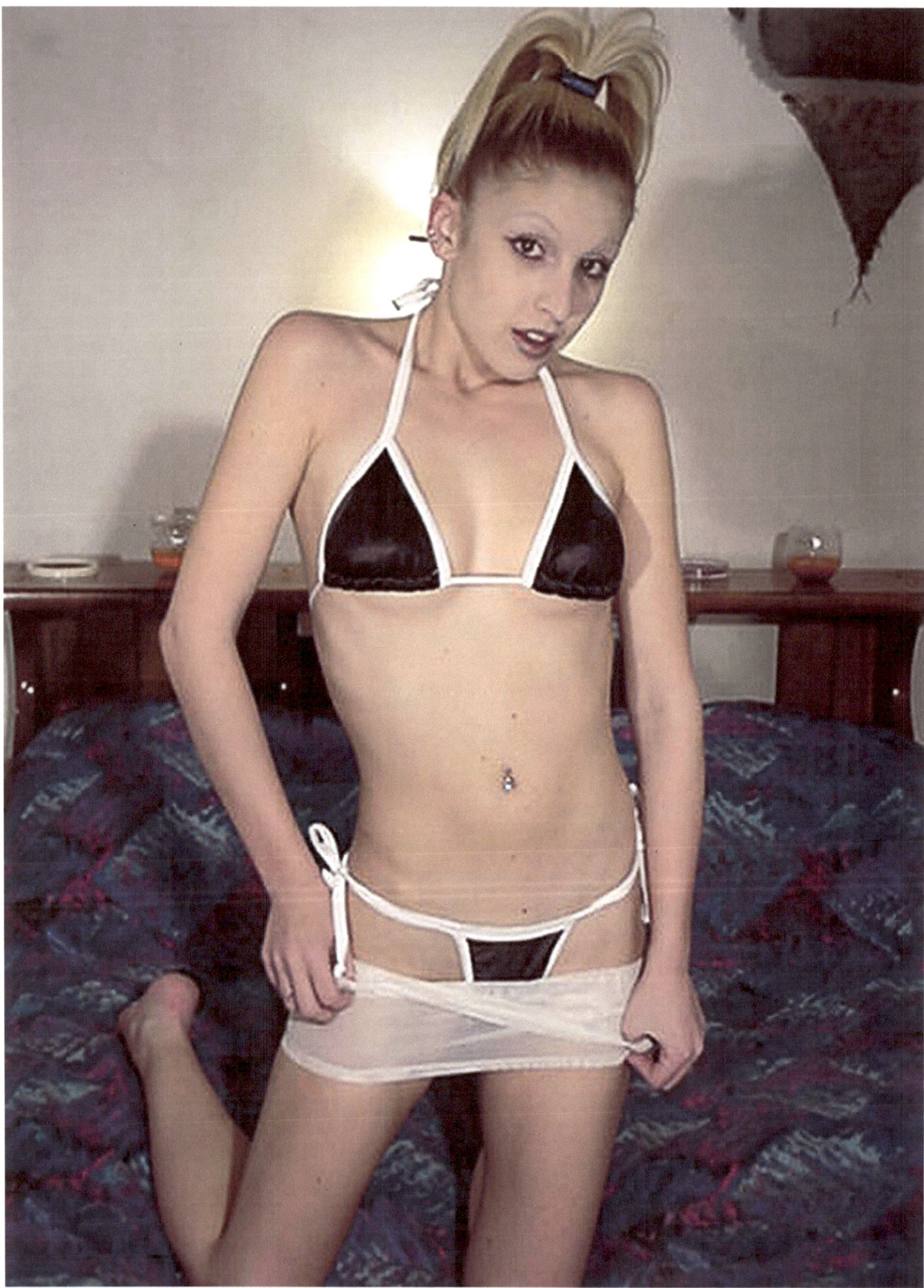

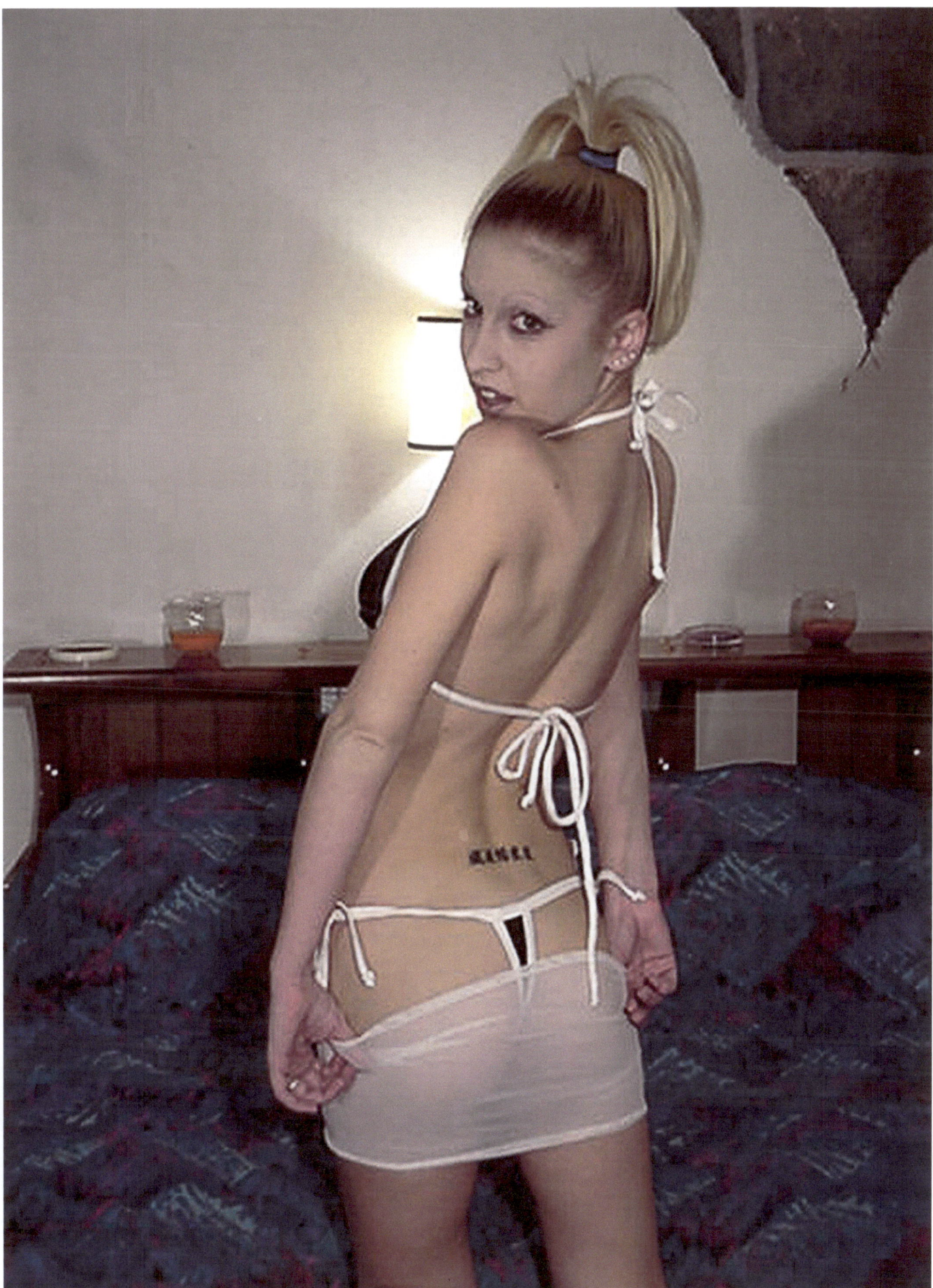

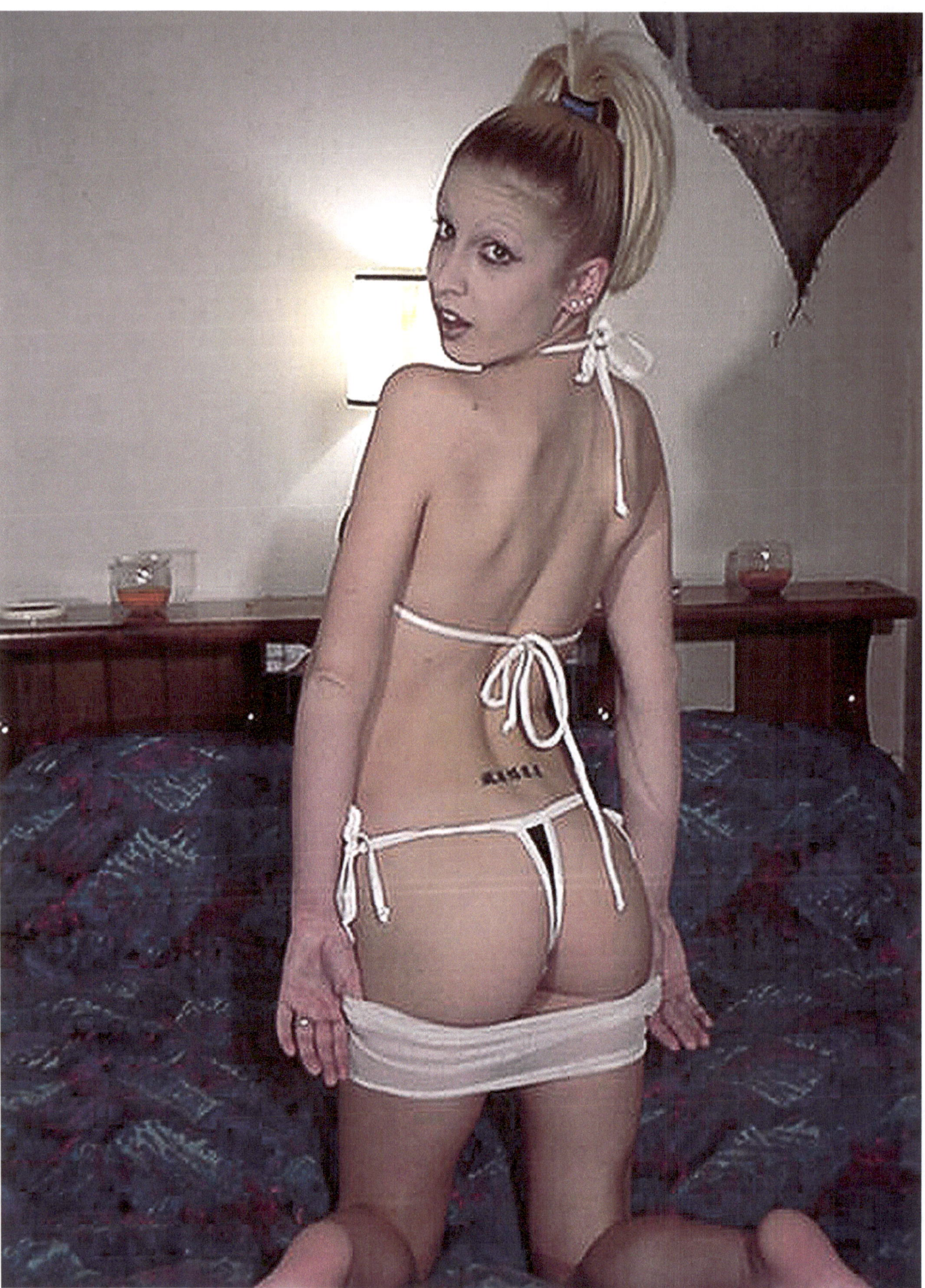

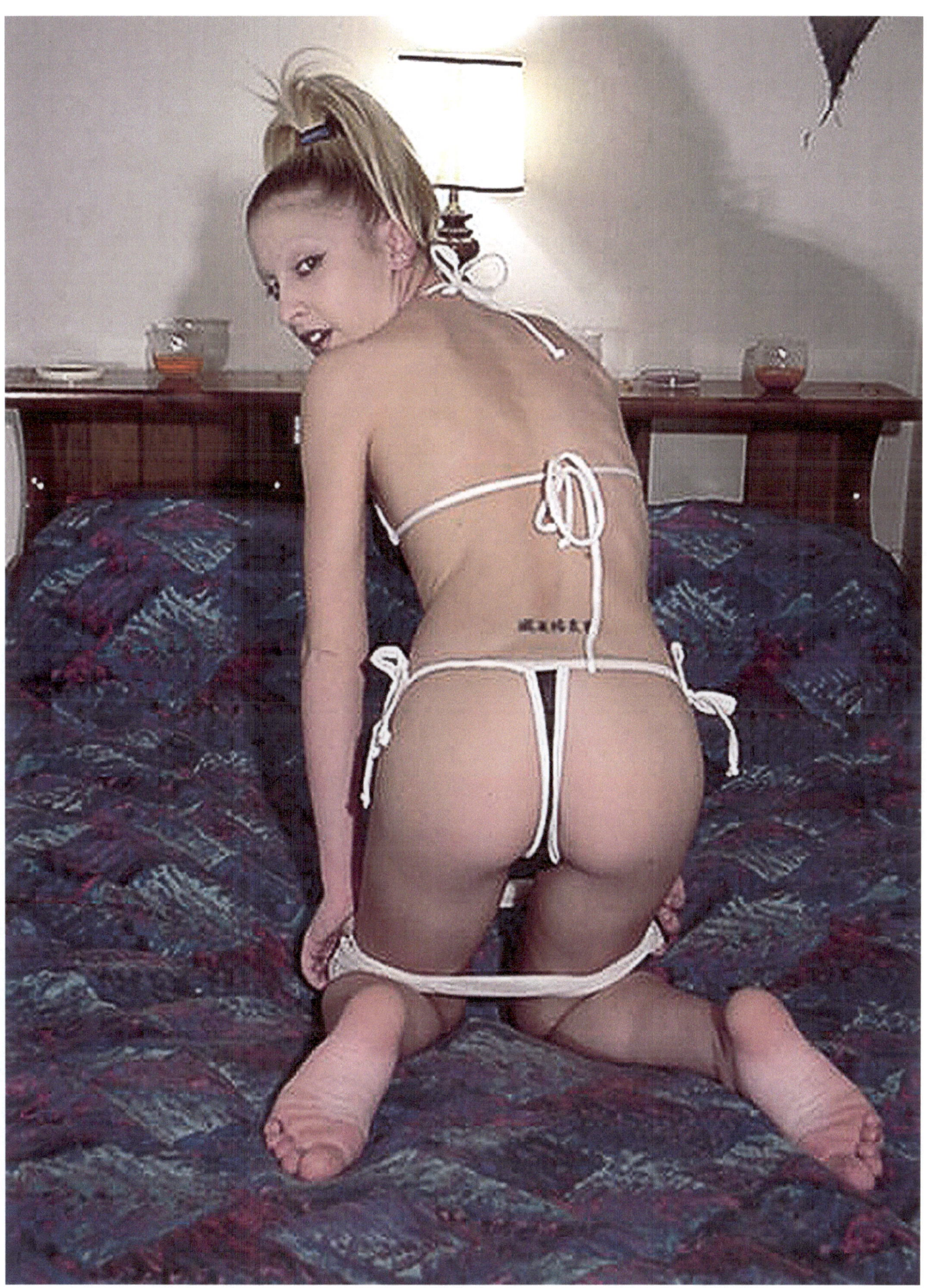

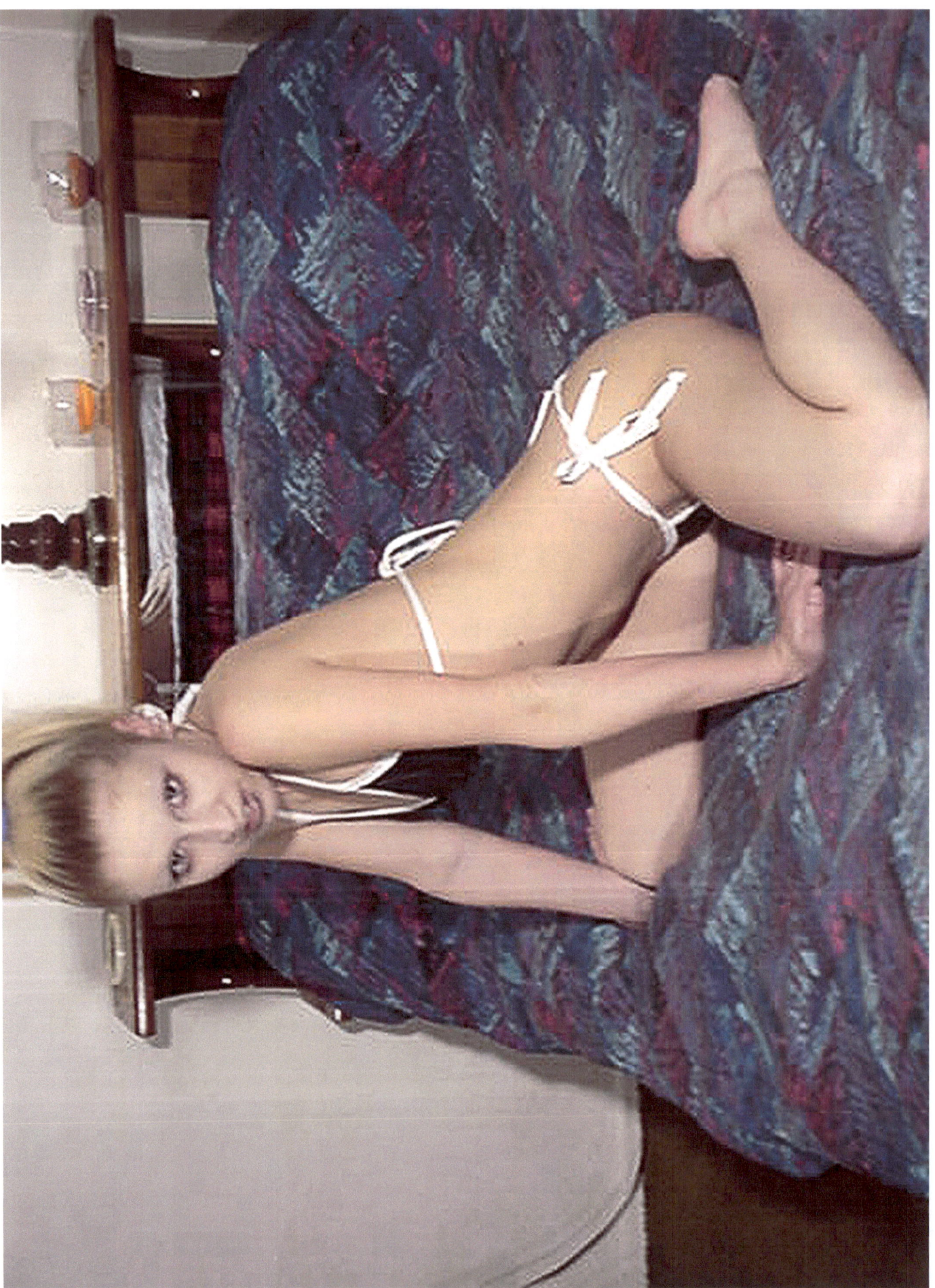

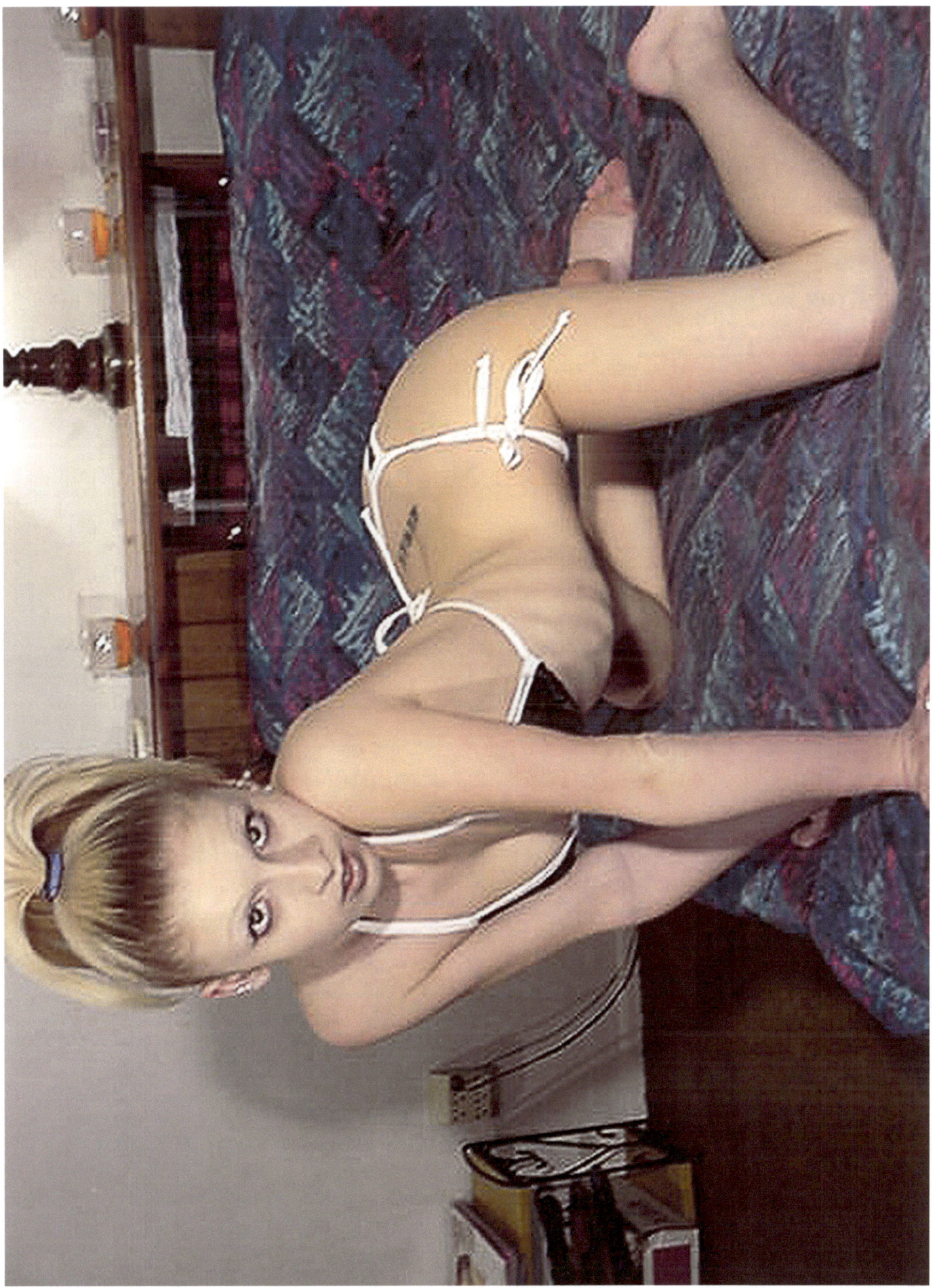

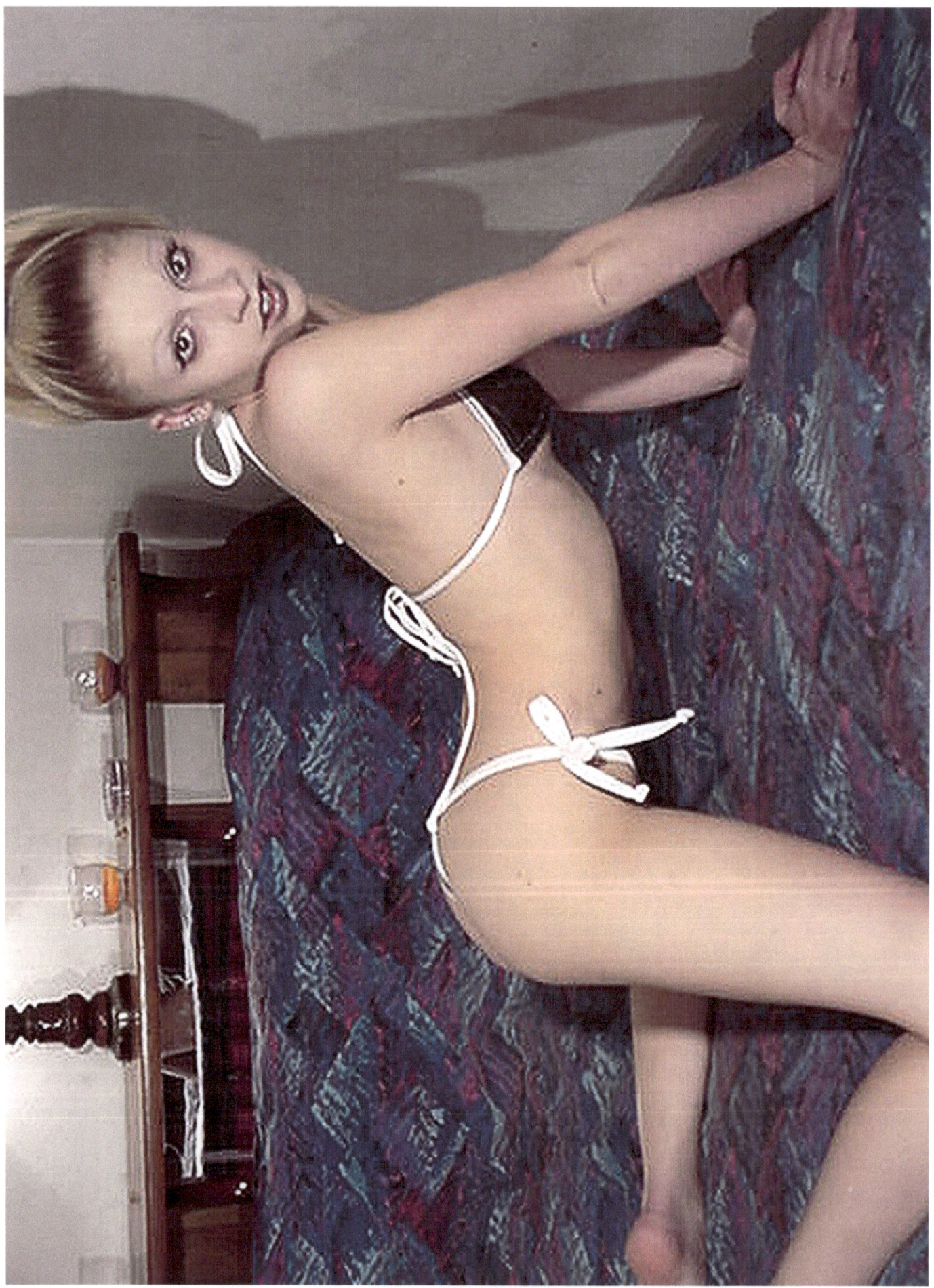

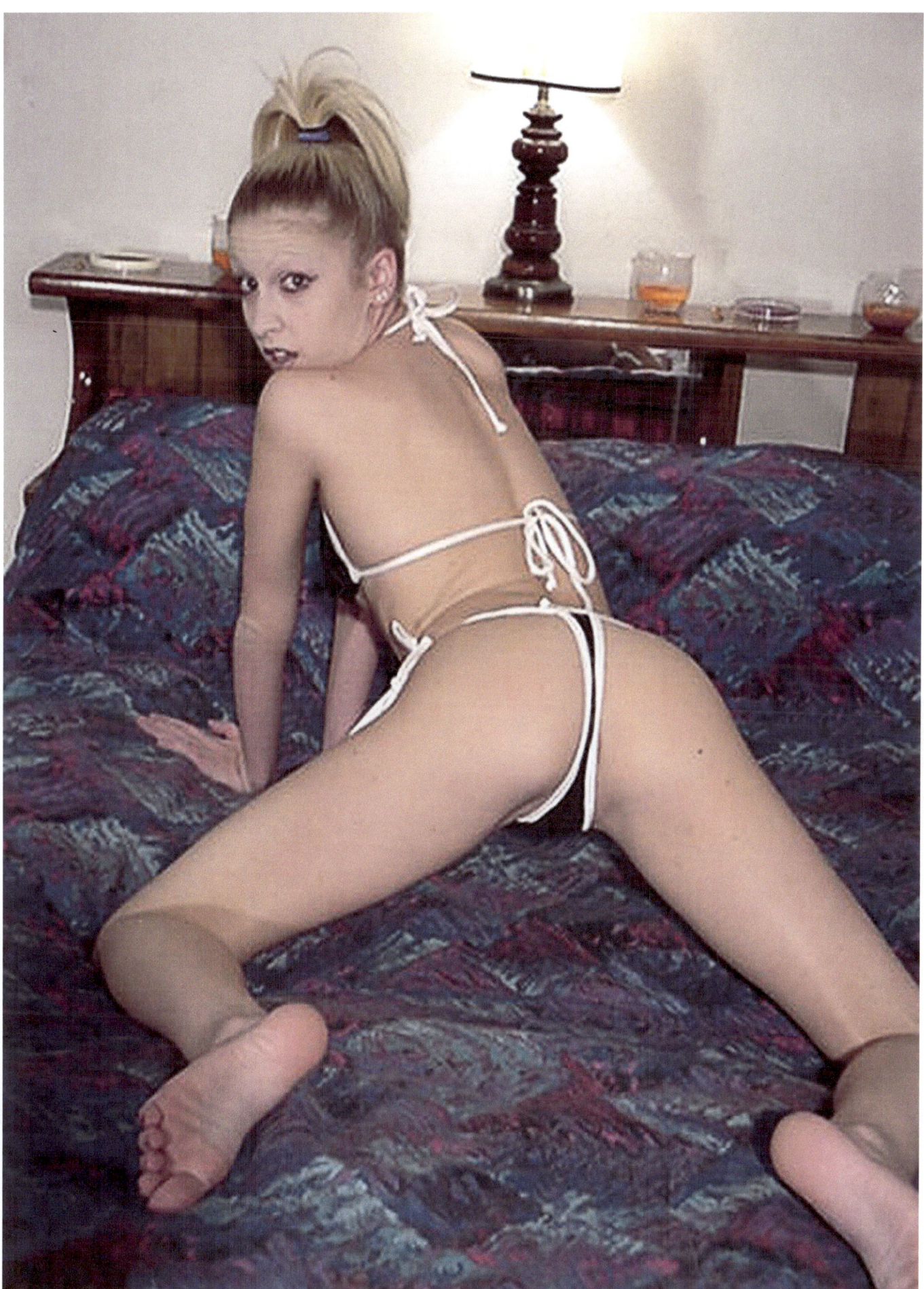

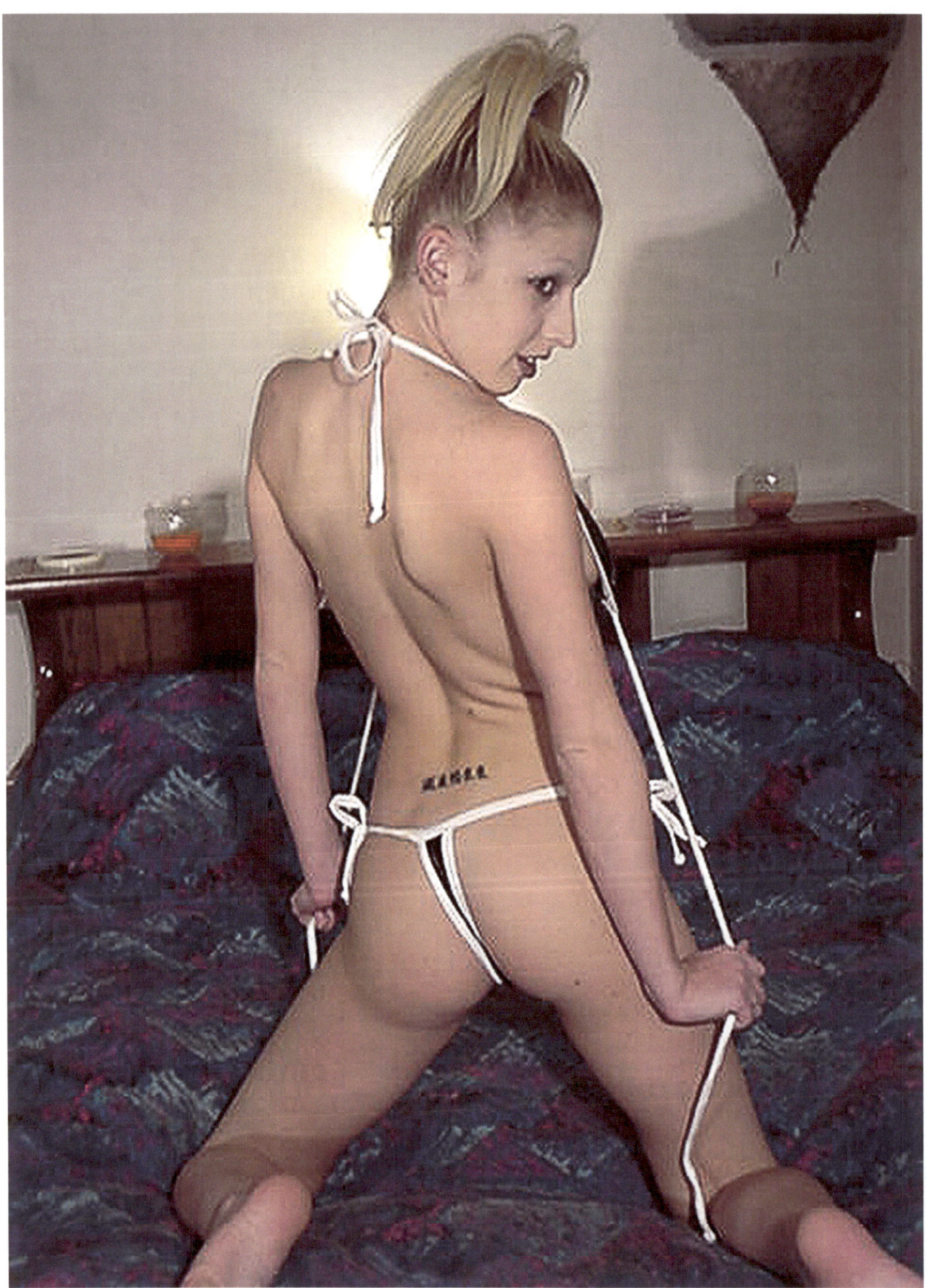

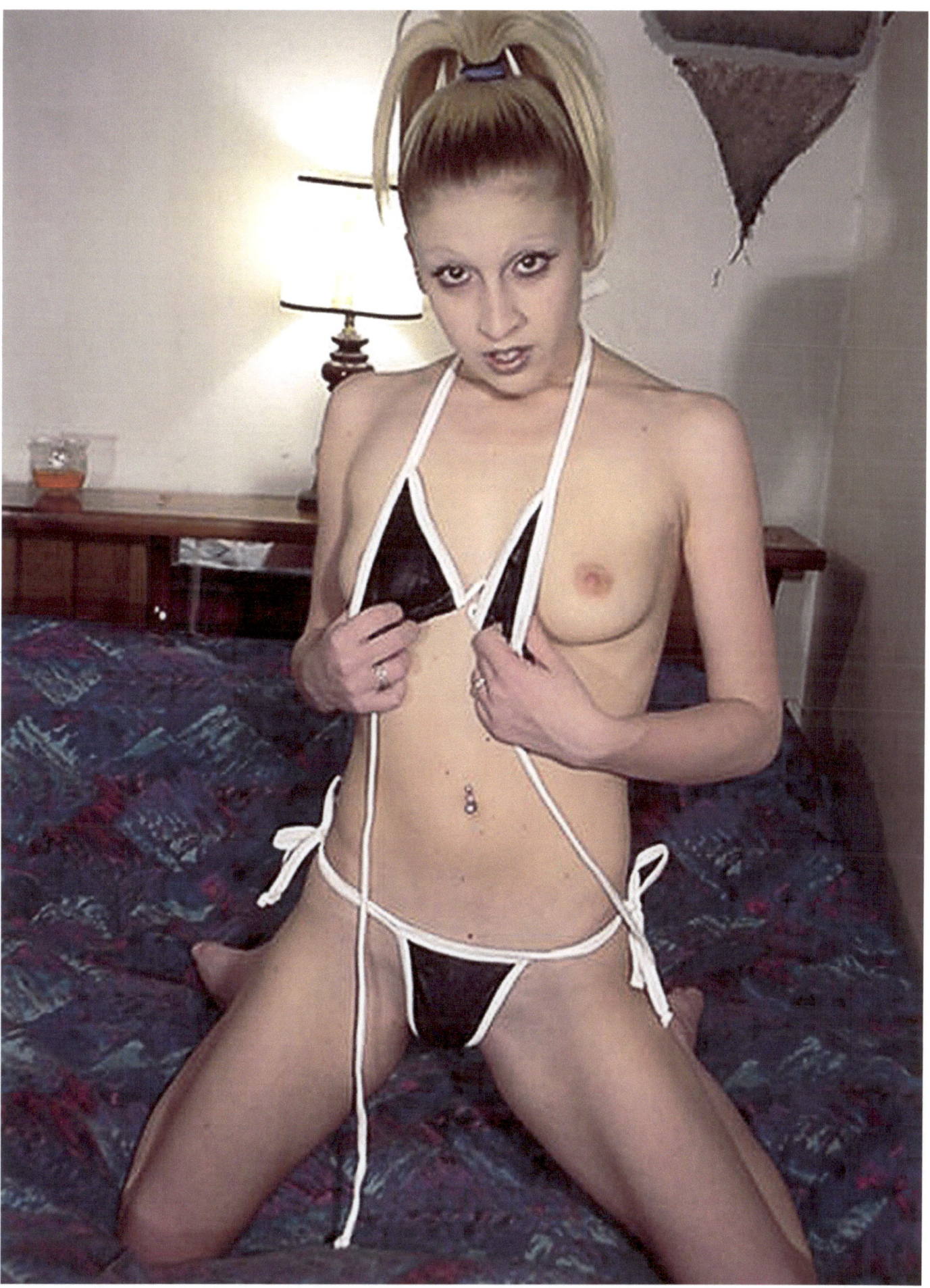

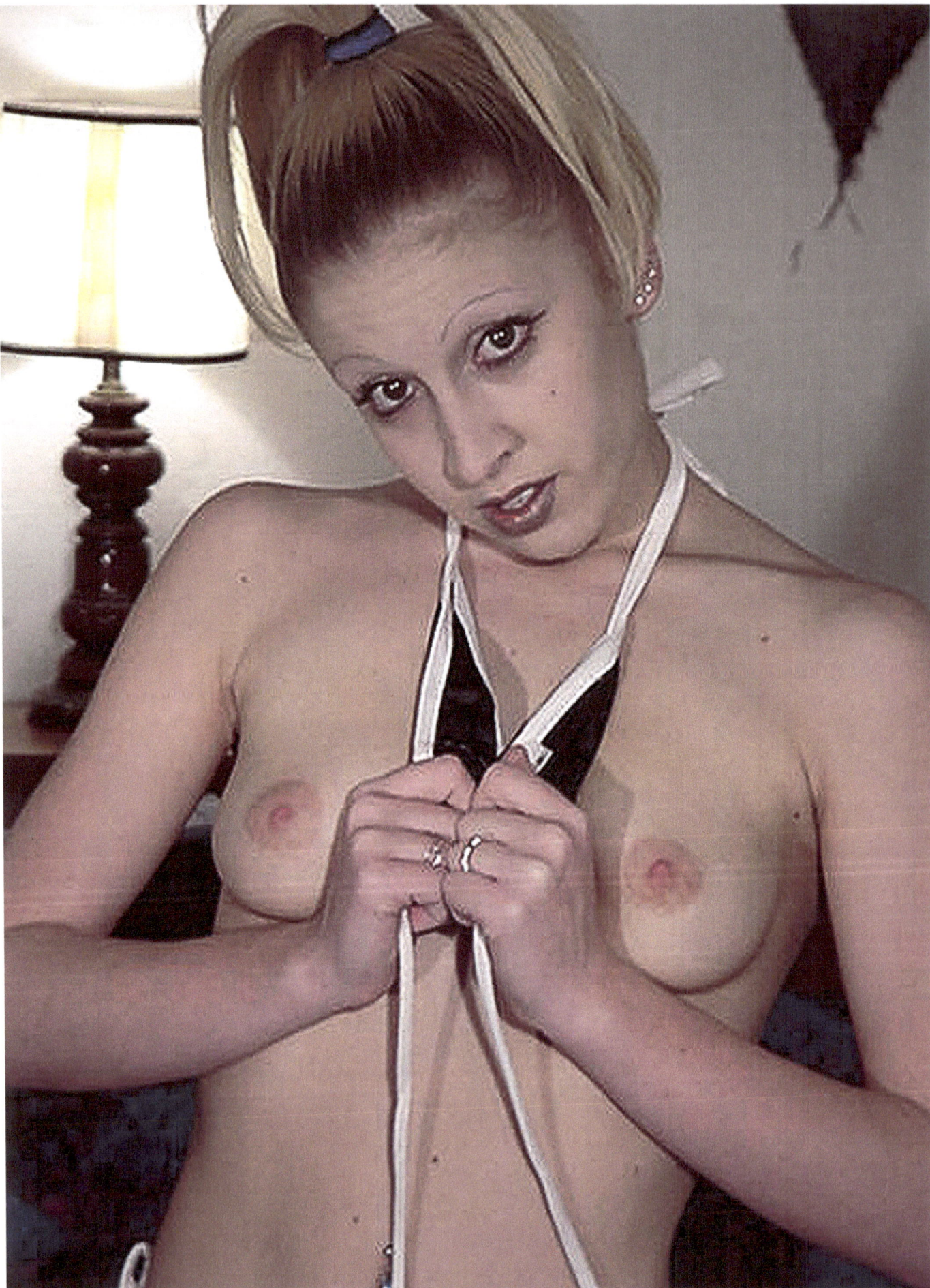

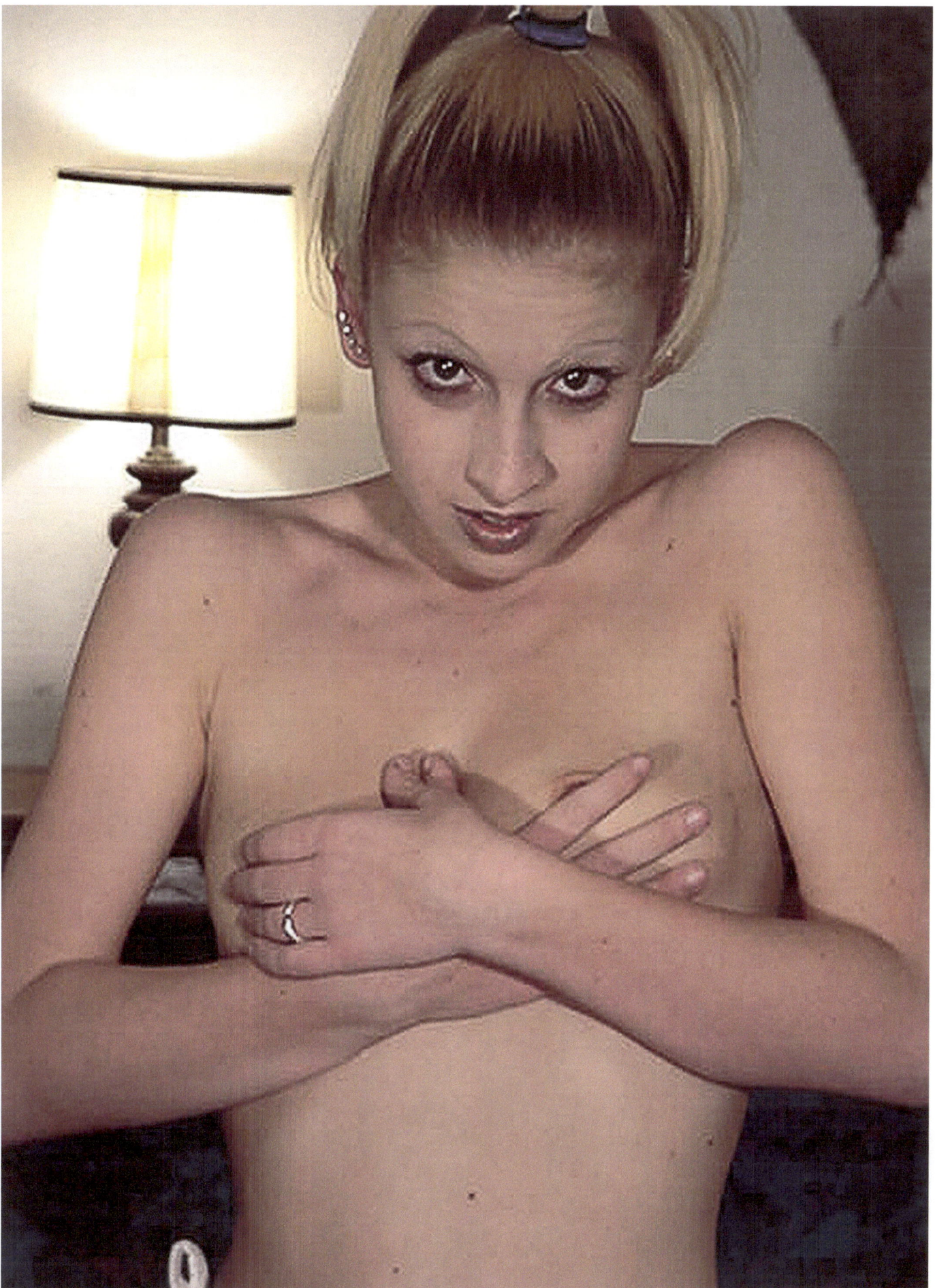

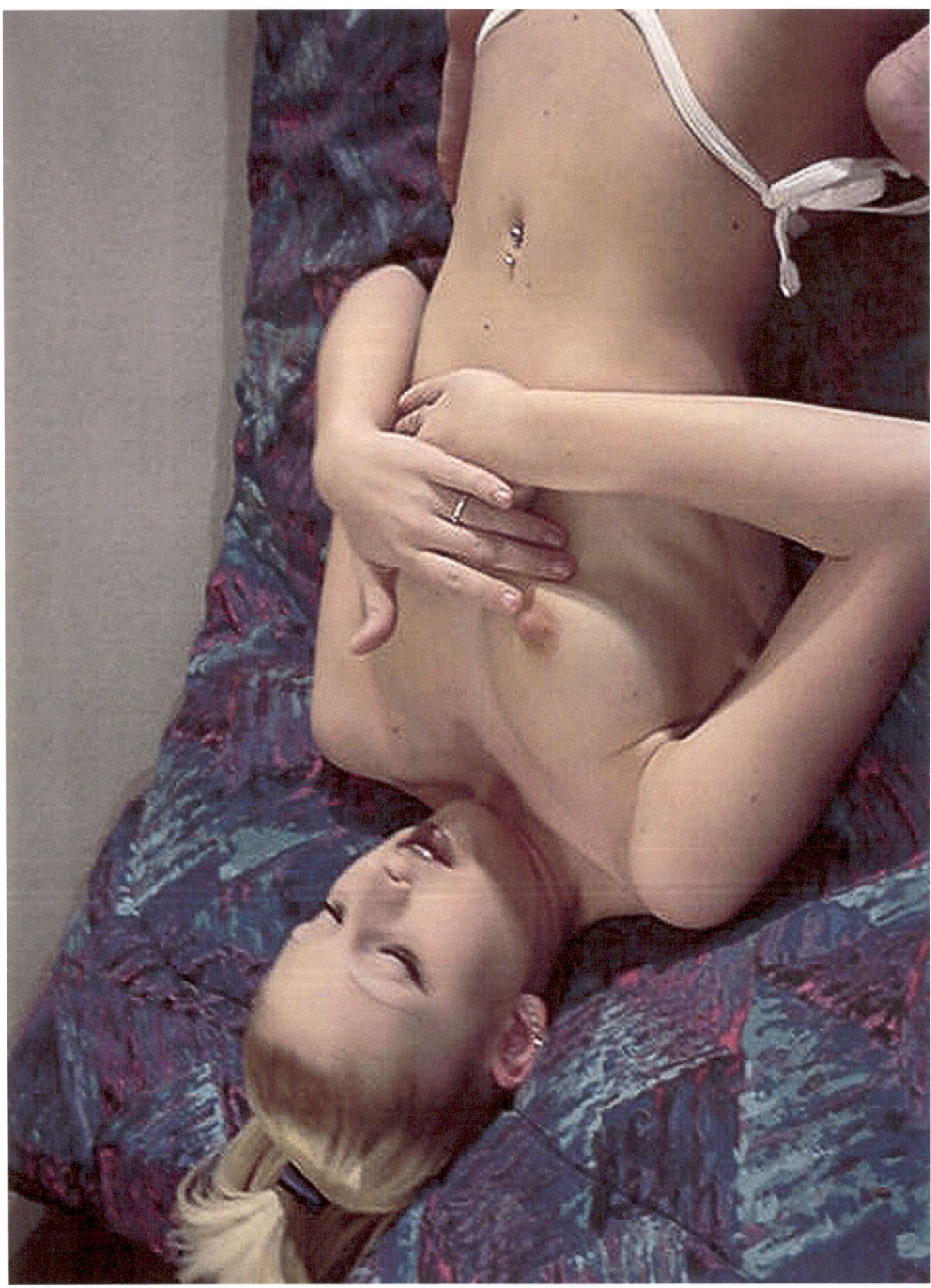

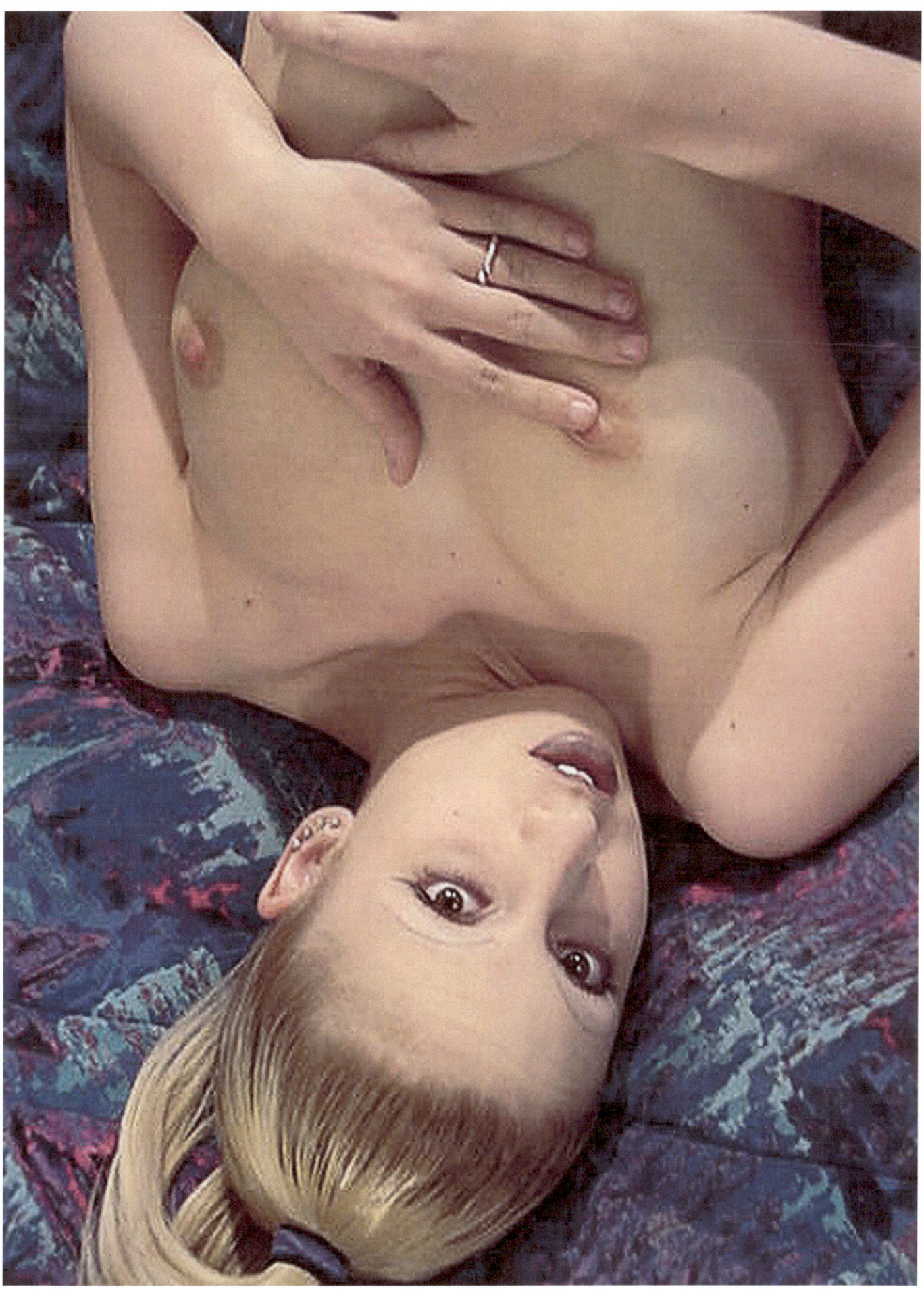

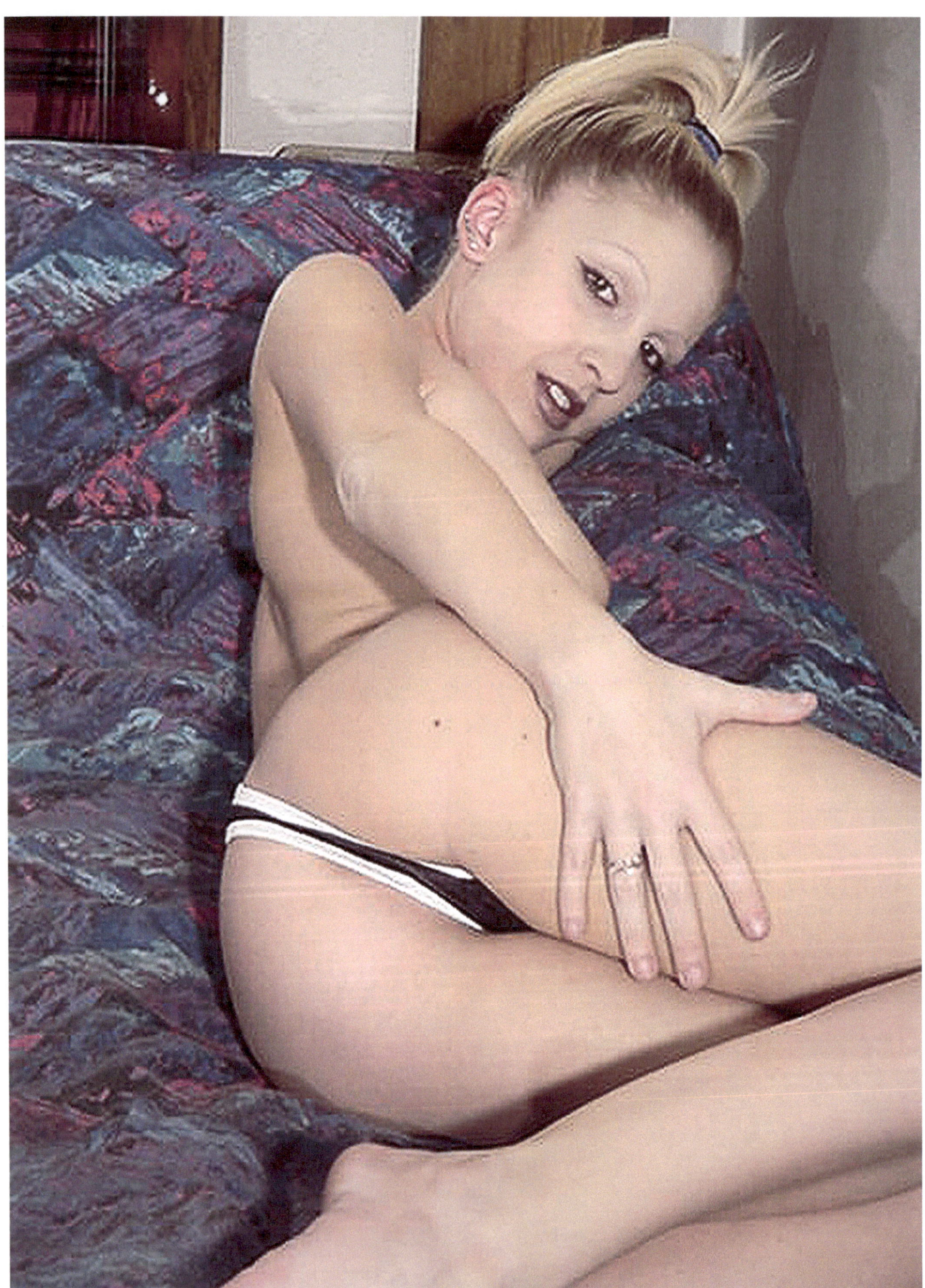

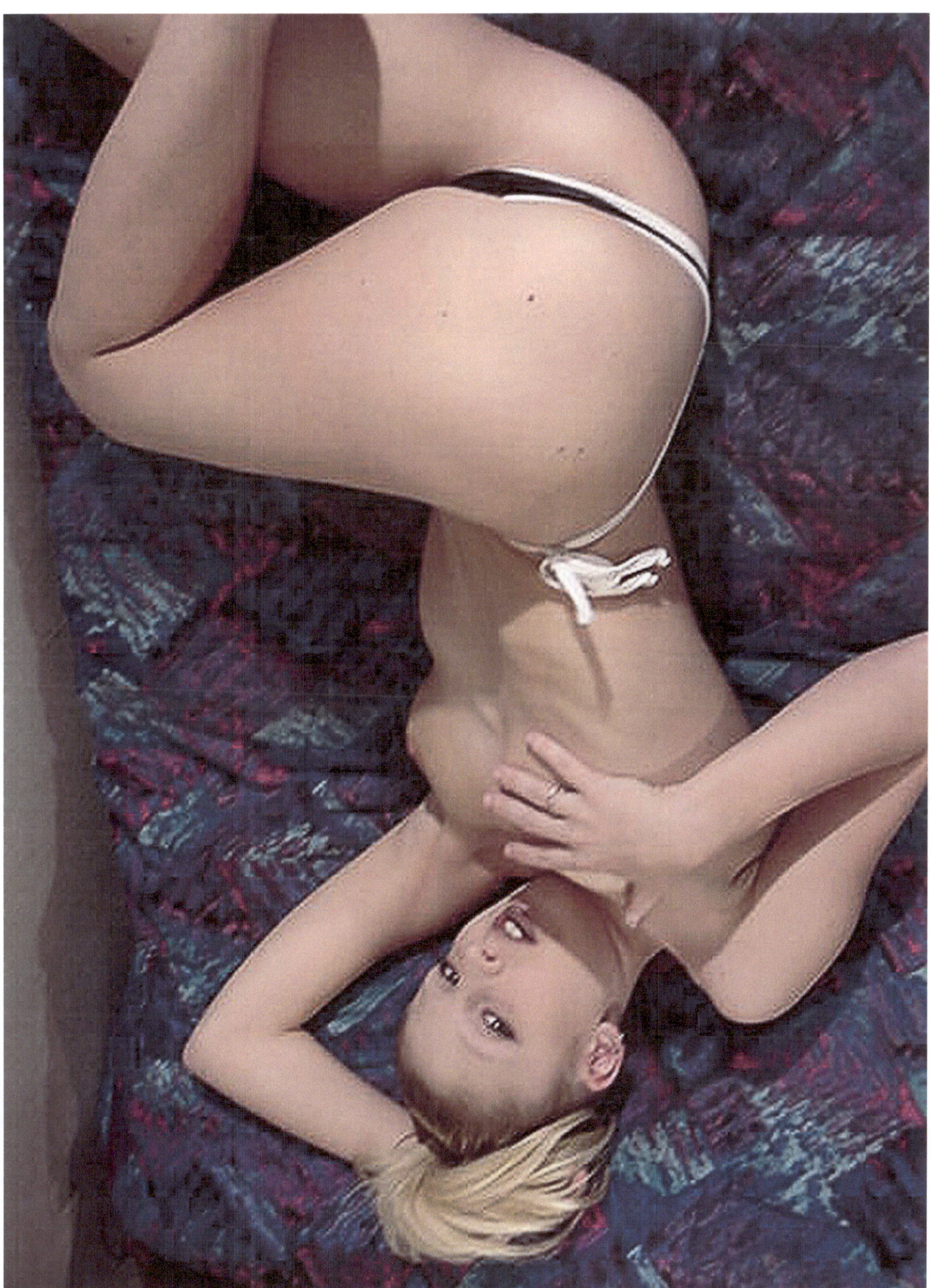

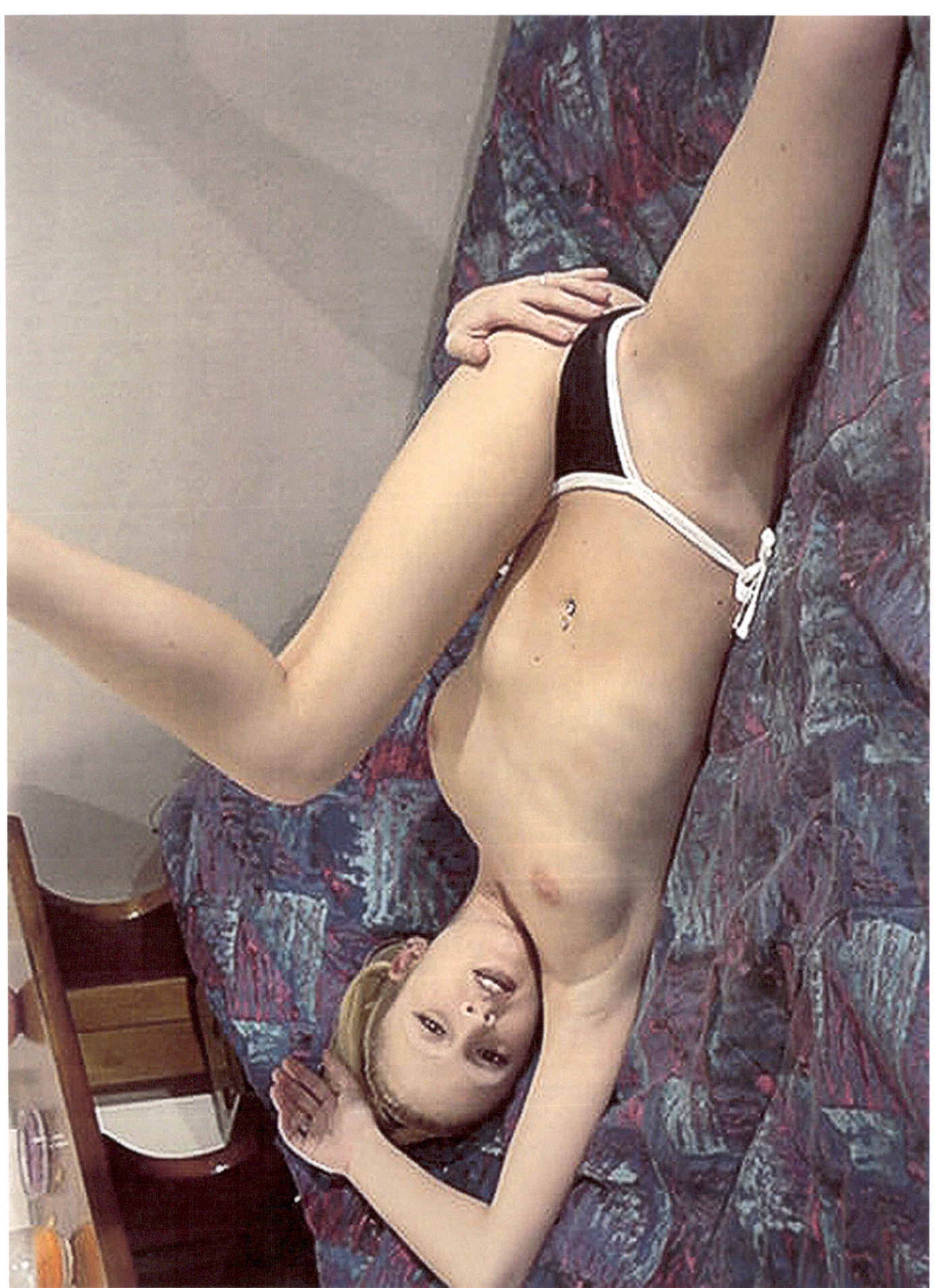

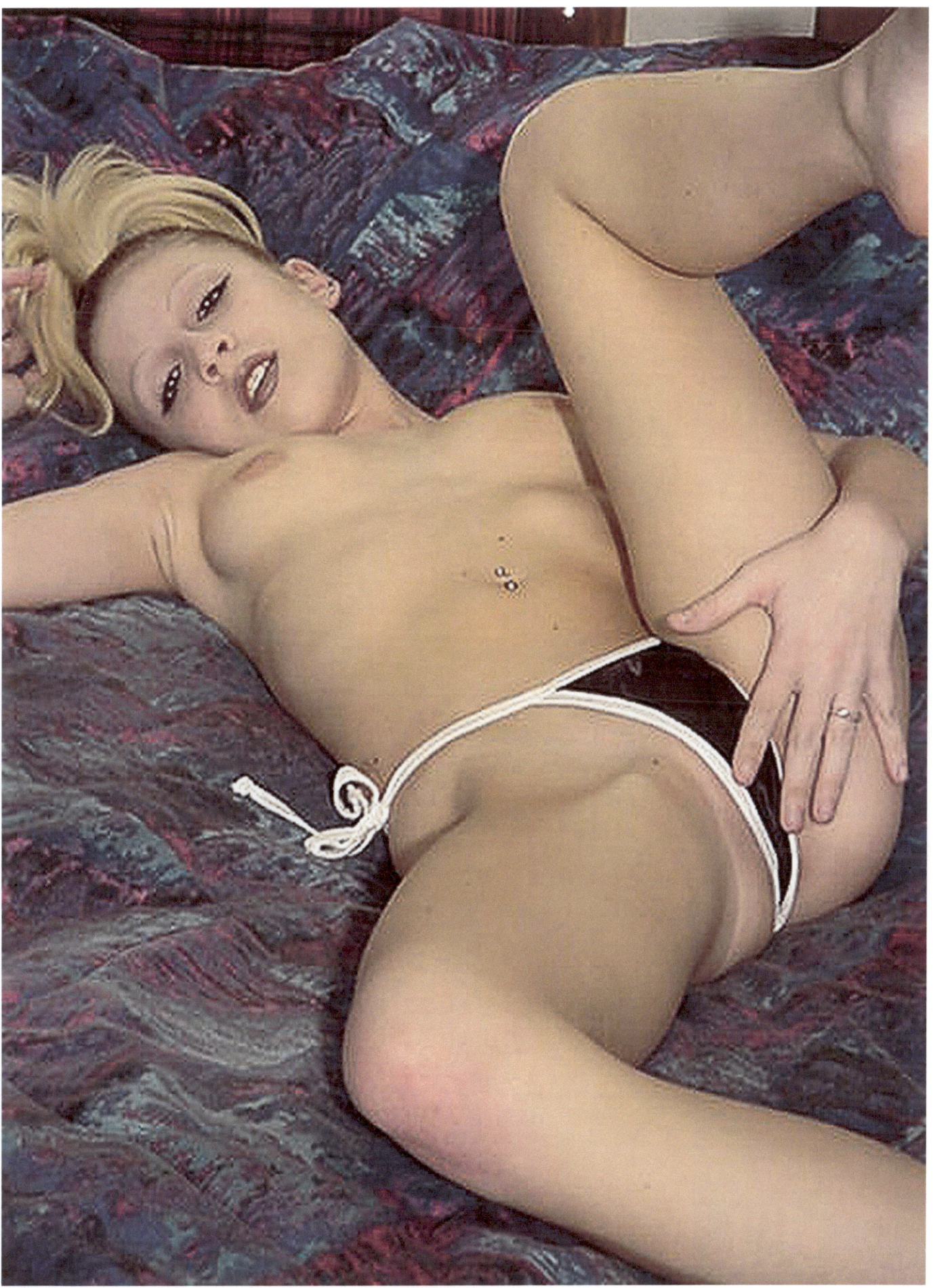

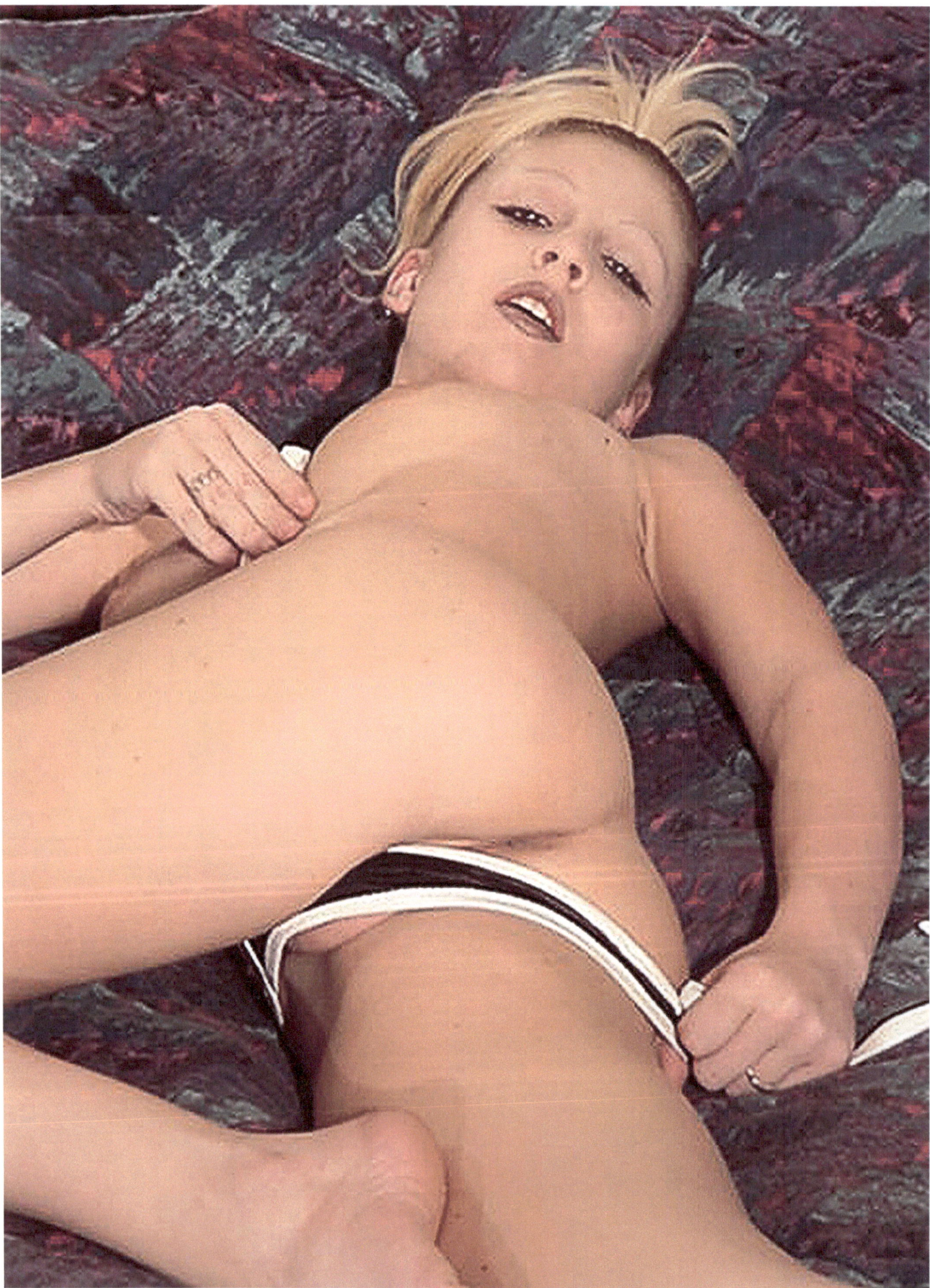

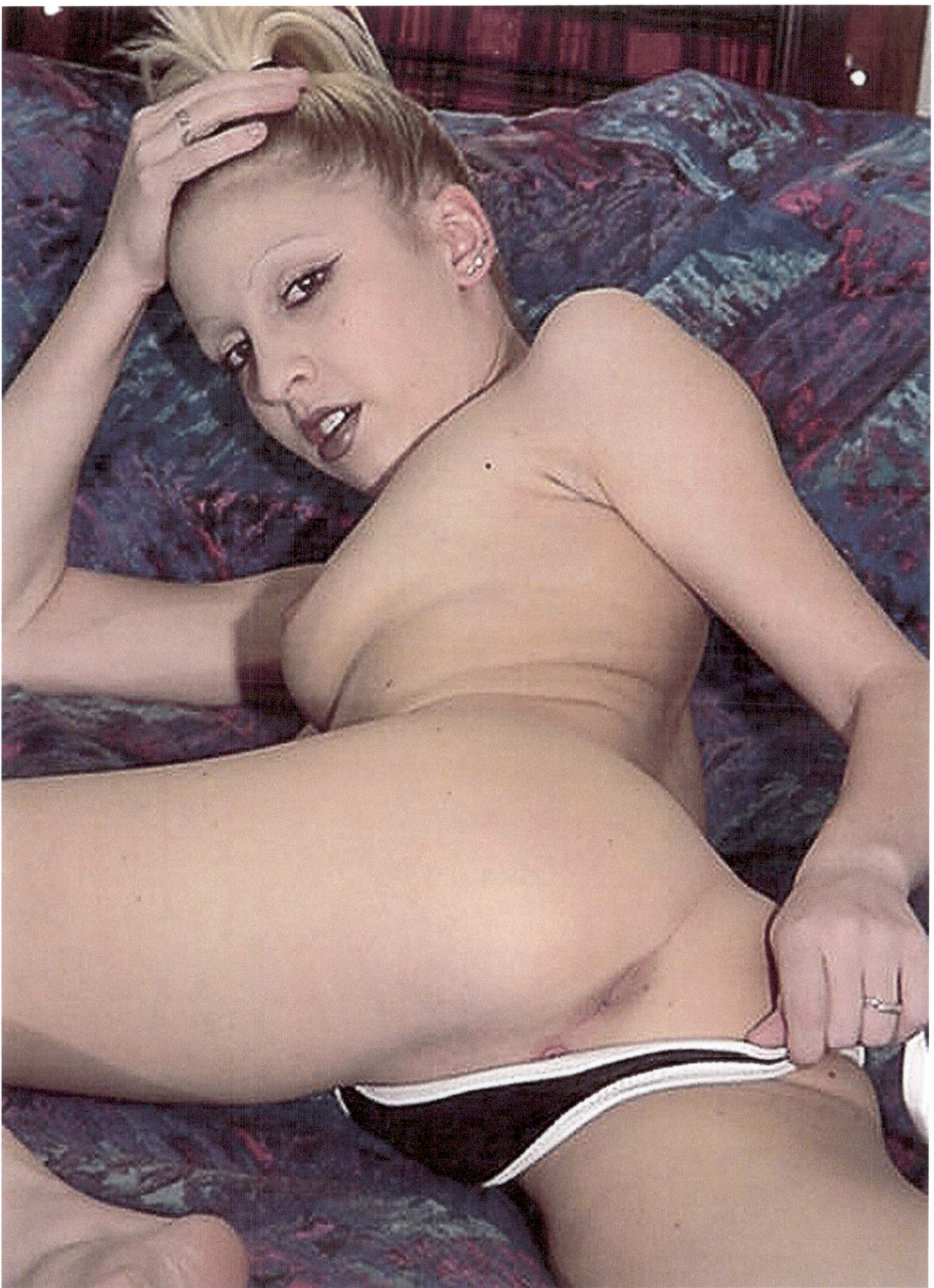

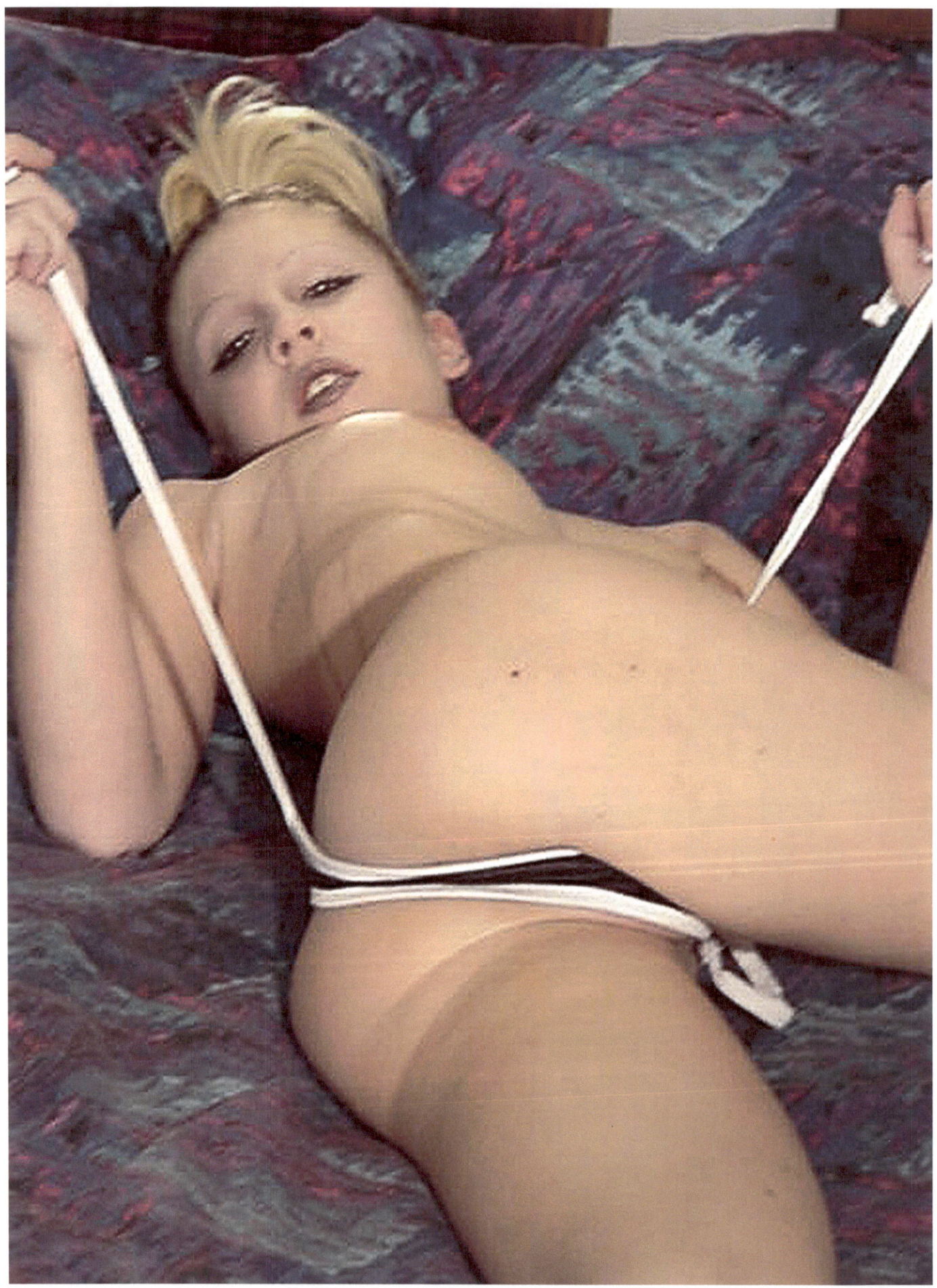

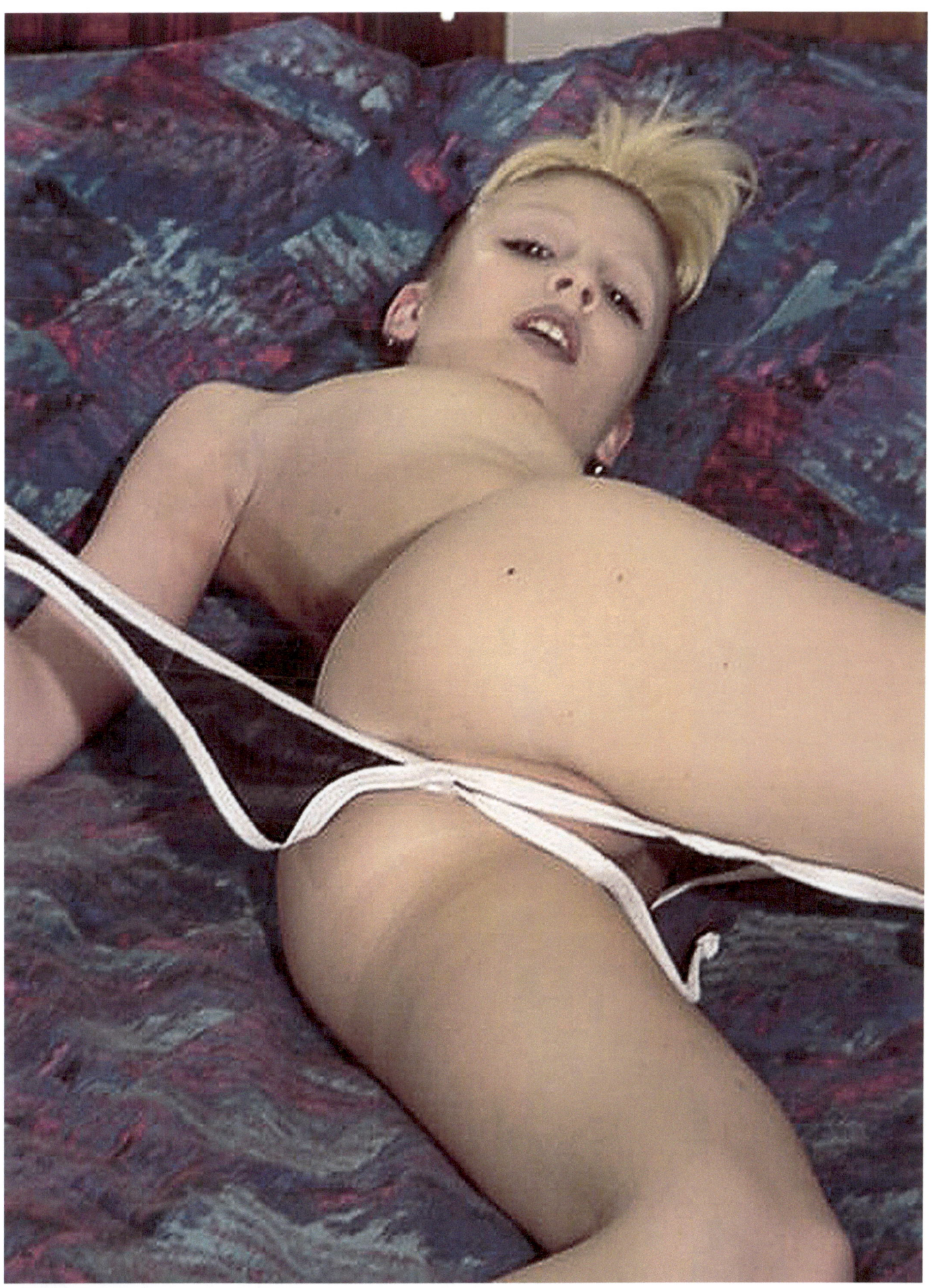

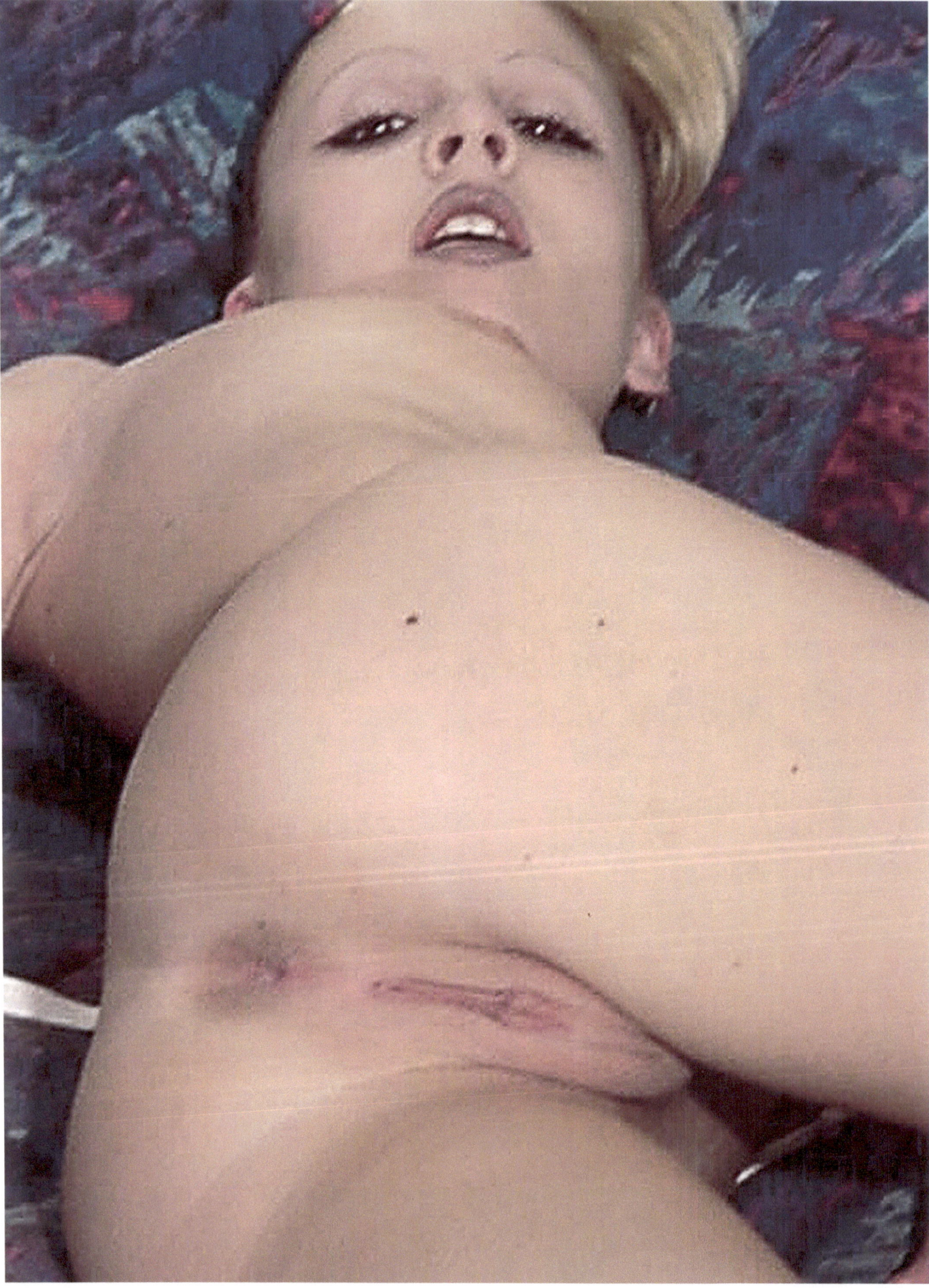

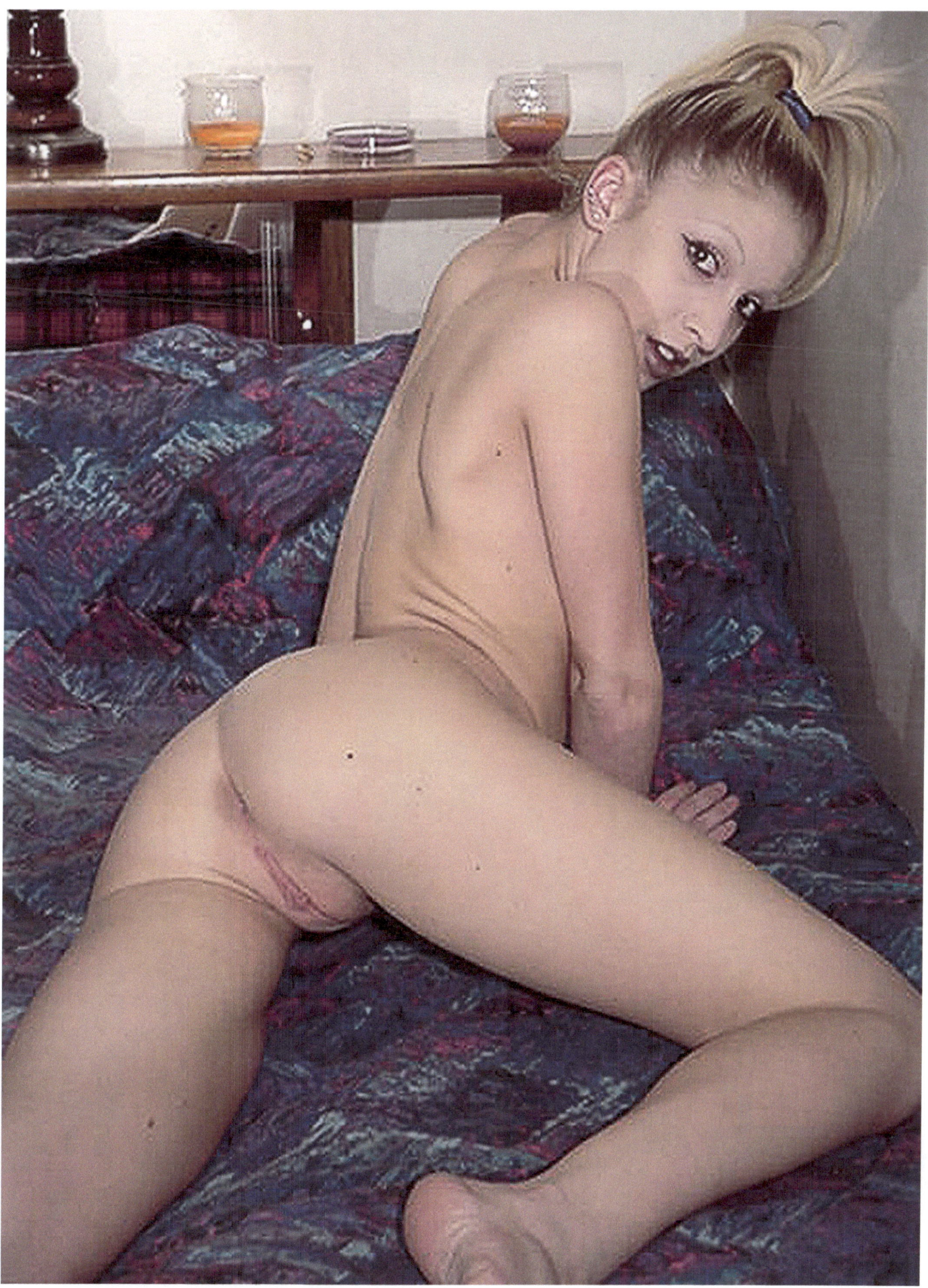

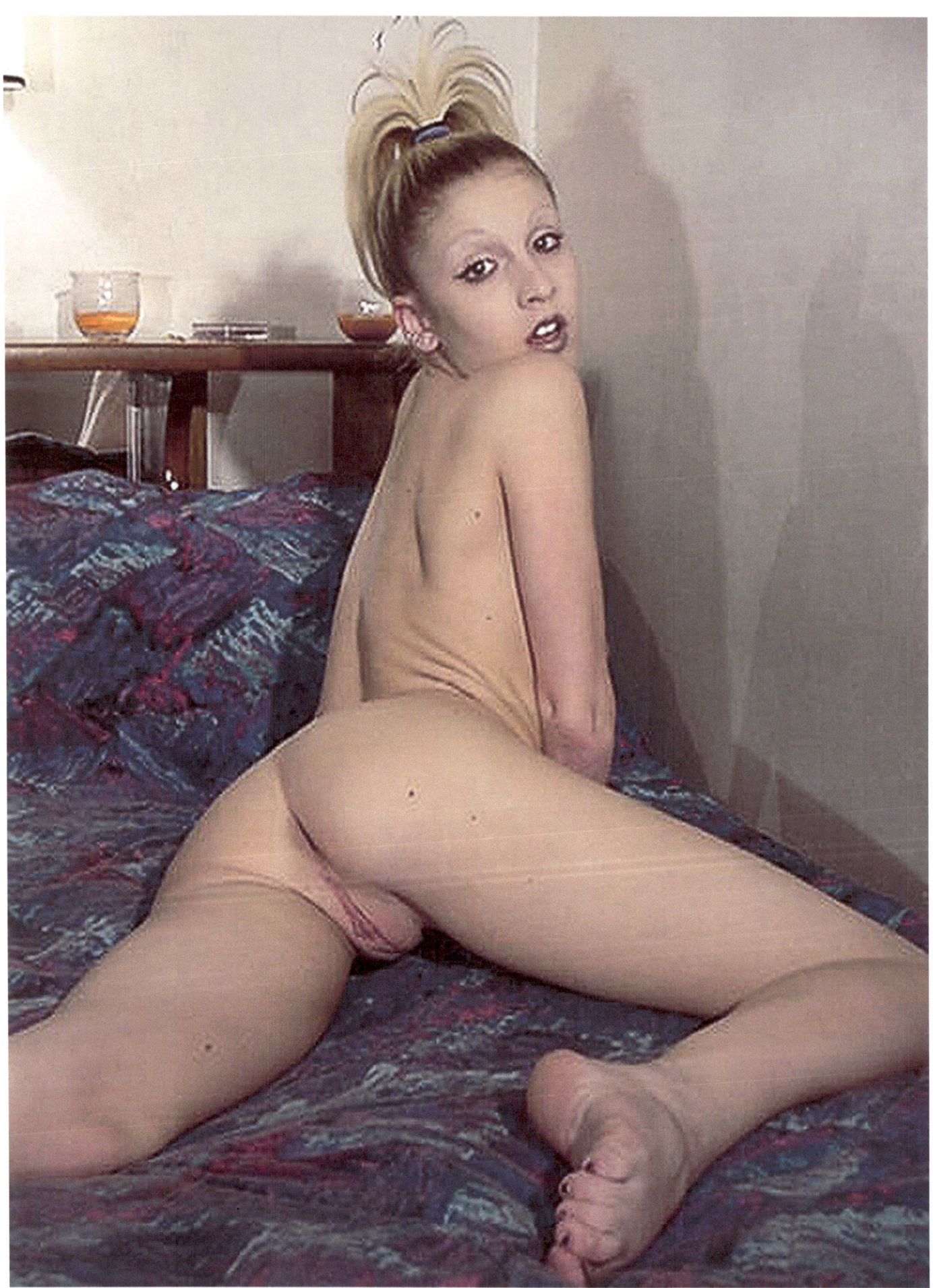

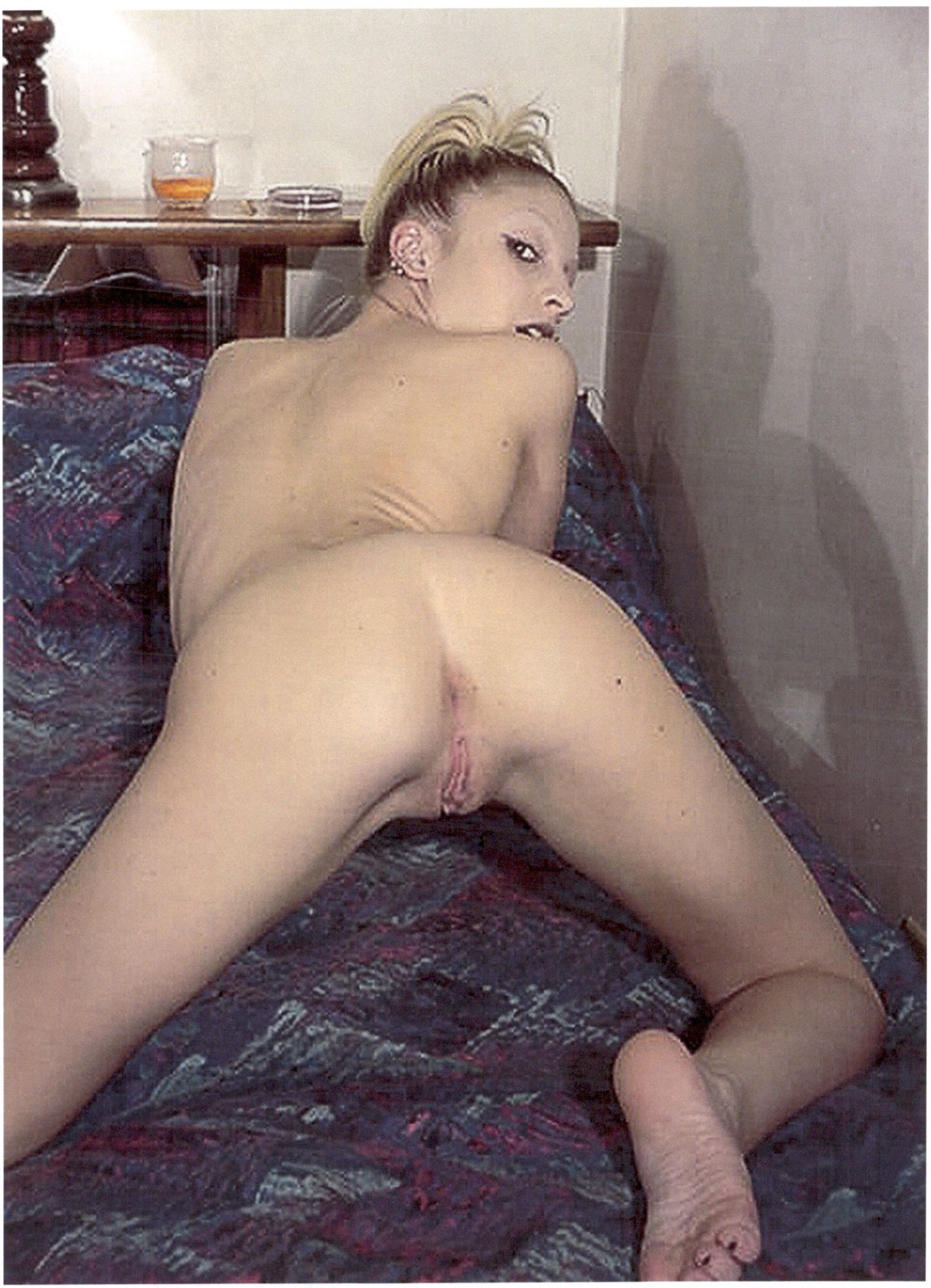

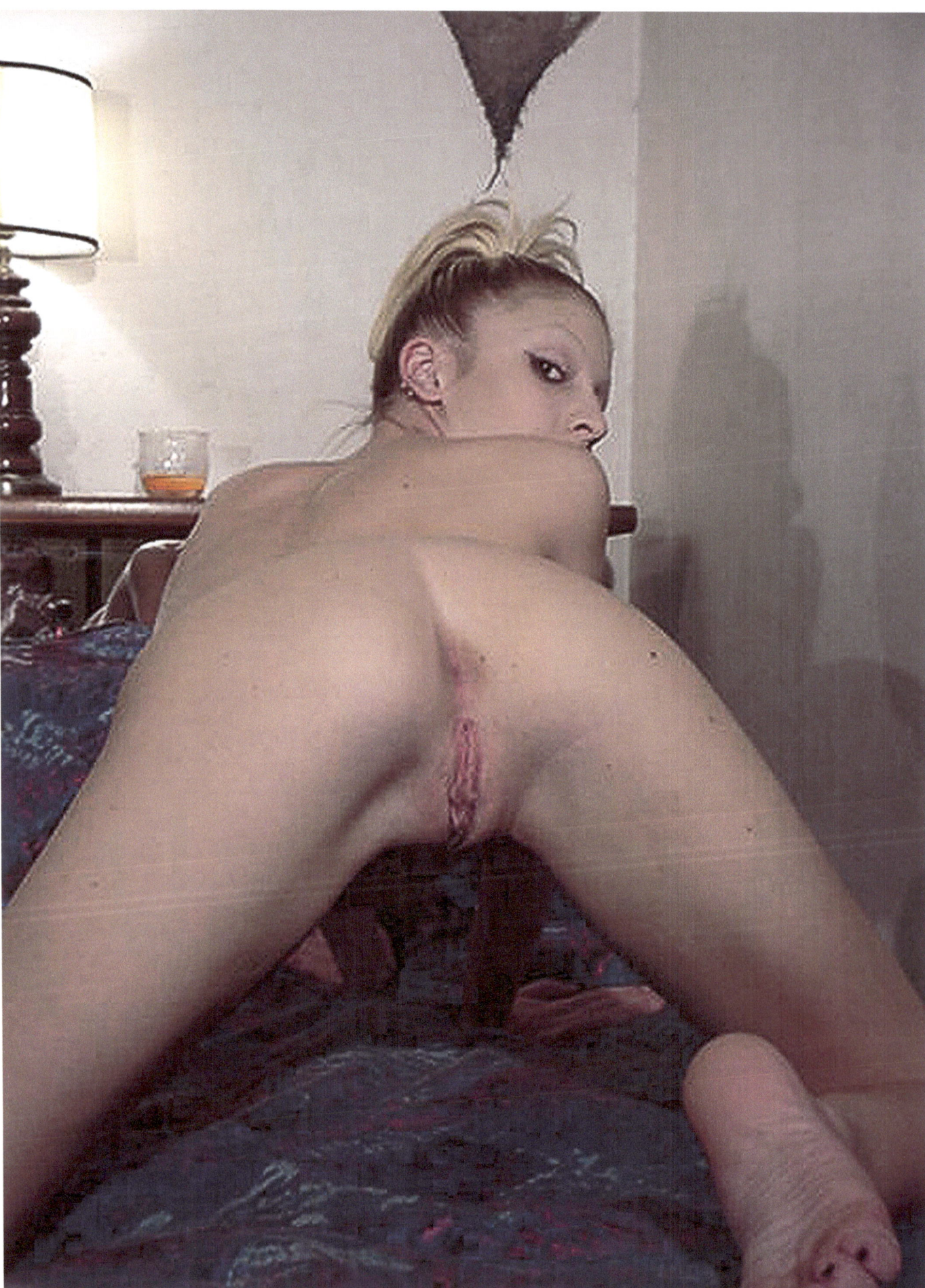

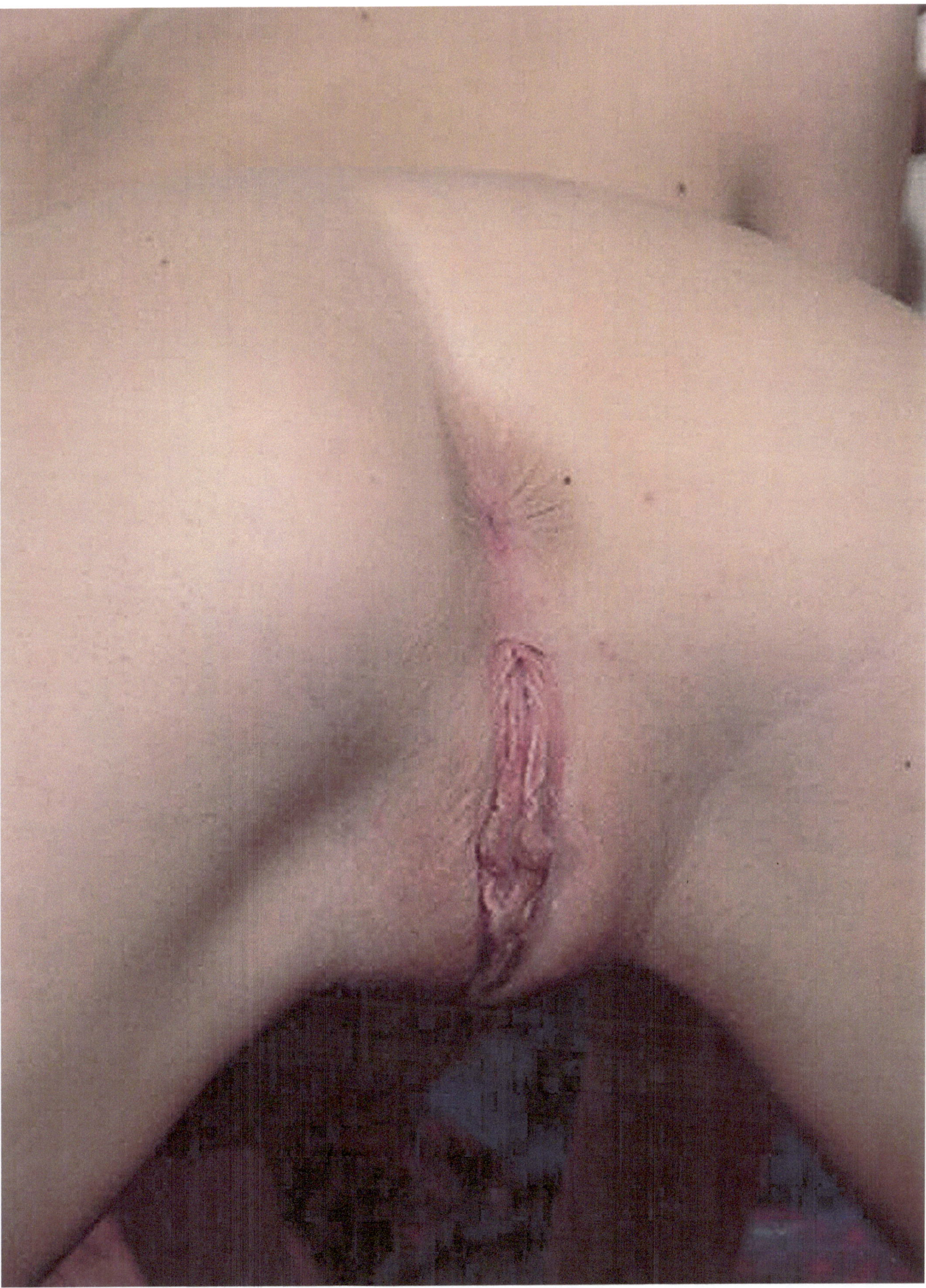

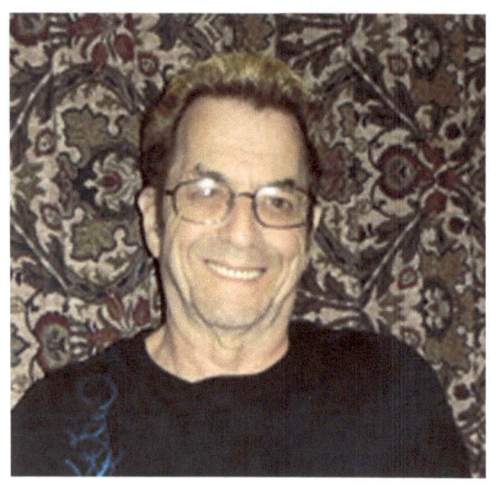

About the Artist and Author!

Peter Dickem, born Sept. 11, 1937, is the oldest working male performer in the adult industry today. Born in Boston Mass. and growing up in Providence, R. I. He moved to Phoenix, Az. In 1989 and still resides there.

He has spent over 35 years as a world famous tattoo artist and at one point owned 3 tattoo shops. He is now retired from tattooing and is devoting all his time to photography.

He started photographing nudes and erotica in 2000 and has been photographing and video taping beautiful women in both nude and erotic adult content for his web sites and for other web sites.

He now has 4 active adult web sites. www.peterdickem.com, www.amateurdreamers.com, www.candypixxx.com and www.oralarizona.com.

www.ingramcontent.com/pod-product-compliance
Lightning Source LLC
Chambersburg PA
CBHW050356180526
45159CB00005B/2043